The Best from
The Bell
Great Irish Writing

Edited by Sean McMahon

ROWMAN AND LITTLEFIELD
TOTOWA, NEW JERSEY

First Published 1978
The O'Brien Press Ltd.
11 Clare Street, Dublin 2, Ireland
First Published in the United States 1979
By Rowman and Littlefield, Totowa, N.J.

ISBN 0-8476-6152-0

Cover design: Jacques Telueur
Binding: J.F. Newman Ltd.
Typesetting: Redsetter Ltd.
Printed in Republic of Ireland by
Folens Printing Co. Ltd.

Published with the assistance of
the Arts Council, Dublin and
the Arts Council of Northern Ireland

FOR DAVID MARCUS

CONTENTS

INTRODUCTION

By SEAN McMAHON

AN institution as significant and as influential as *The Bell* really demands a book-length history and is inevitably very poorly served by an introduction as brief as this. That history should it ever come to be written would have a lot to say as well about the Ireland of the Forties and early Fifties; for if ever a magazine held the mirror up to nature and showed Ireland her own face, *The Bell* did. This was due, partly to the nature of the journal, as envisioned by its editors, Sean O'Faolain and Peadar O'Donnell, and partly because its seed happened to fall upon unusually fertile ground.

It began its tinkling in October 1940 and except for a gap of two and a half years, from April 1948 until November 1950, and an occasional stagger towards the end of its life, it appeared monthly until December 1954. At times the tinkle became a clang as the magazine made the headlines. It was never banned but from time to time the odd exasperated politician or choleric churchman criticised it and once or twice denounced it. Like most worthwhile things in the country it was declared anti-Irish and in the early days at least tended to have an under-the-counter sale in the smaller towns down the country. Occasionally printers exercised their opportunity to censor and county librarians used indulge in a little unofficial scissoring as when in Cork Public Library some art pages which reproduced paintings of nudes were neatly removed before the magazine was displayed on the stand. On the whole its prestige grew and former enemies tended as time went by to cherish it as the bold child of the family is cherished.

Much of the success of *The Bell* was due to its editors. O'Faolain served (in every sense especially the laborious one) from the beginning till April 1946, a period of exactly six and a half years, O'Donnell saw it through the remaining forty-three issues. It is impossible to imagine *The Bell* without these two men, it simply could not have happened without them. Though very different in personality, in political creed and in their careers, they were sufficiently at one in their vision of what *The Bell* should do and were as complementary as was necessary to make sure it did it. One excellent anthology of *Bell* material would be the collected editorials of these men. They wrote well and challengingly about all aspects of Irish life and kept the campanile echoing. (The title which has given rise to all kinds of campanological jokes through the years had at the beginning no especial significance as O'Faolain wrote in his first editorial:

> Any other equally spare and hard and simple word would have done: any word with a minimum of associations.)

While O'Faolain was editor, Peadar O'Donnell contributed much material and handled the business side of the enterprise. Then after 1946 when O'Donnell took over the chair O'Faolain still contributed stories, reviews, articles and one famous counterblast against the Bishop of Galway, which is included in this selection. His view of the magazine was as a kind of house journal for the isolated and earnest country. He sought new writers, encouraged them when he found them, taught them by frequent re-editing and established in them a rare professionalism. Yet though original creative writing was to form the bulk of the material, it was not to be an exclusively literary journal like *Scrutiny* or *Penguin New Writing* (both contemporaries). Thus though the young writers were invited, as Frank O'Connor urged from 'The Belfry' (in the first number) 'to benefit from occasional abuse' as they ran the gauntlet of his criticism, and though the magazine also contained the usual sections devoted to art, theatre, cinema and book criticism, many of the articles were what we might clumsily call 'sociological' which showed the country working.

Flann O'Brien contributed early articles on 'Going to the Dogs', 'The "Trade" in Dublin' and 'The Dance Halls'. Eileen O'Faolain, the editor's wife did a piece in the fourth issue on 'Galway Hats' and followed it two years later, in December 1943, with an article on 'Silk Stockings', incidentally introducing Irish readers to the new man-made wonder, Nylon, and using what must be the longest if not the wickedest word in all of *The Bell's* 131 issues, 'polyhexamethyleneadipamide'. Norah McGuinness, the artist, contributed an article on window dressing. Everything well-written and relevant was suitable. Life in Ireland at the time was in O'Faolain's words 'pretty deadly dull'. The war in Europe, neutrality with its isolation and twinges of guilt, the growing-pains of an eighteen-year old state, De Valera's vision of Ireland as part kibbutz and part christian Tara, all led to a general dispiritedness and O'Faolain's hope was that *The Bell* would play some part in jizzing up the sluggish life of the country. Music teachers, psychiatrists, mechanics, nuns and even a convicted felon gave first-hand accounts of their lives — these modified by the suggestions of an endlessly patient editor. He had the right instinct for what topics should be covered and who should best cover them. All in all *The Bell* lived up to the description sometimes printed below the title: 'a survey of Irish life'.

Not all the contributors attracted to the magazine were unknowns. In February 1945 Shaw, O'Casey and T. Kingsmill Moore contributed to a symposium on censorship, which along with Gaelic was one of the buzziest bees in O'Faolain's bonnet, and Monk Gibbon asked for equal space for reply. The Northern counties were unselfconsciously assumed to be part of *The Bell's* country. Many Ulster writers became regular contributors, the issue of July 1941 was one of several Ulster Numbers. The writers either refused to recognize the political border or discounted it in their literary lives. Such people as John Hewitt (under his own name and a pseudonym, John Howard), Roy McFadden, Maurice Craig, Thomas Carnduff, Michael McLaverty, Sam Hanna Bell, W. R. Rodgers and Mary Beckett helped give the magazine its special flavour. Young graduates were encouraged to try their hands at unlikely topics: Vivian Mercier who afterwards wrote *The Irish Comic Tradition* (1962) wrote on Jazz and the Press and included in his survey one famous piece on 'The Six Jokes of *Dublin Opinion*' (December, 1944) and Conor Cruise O'Brien began as 'Donat O'Donnell' a first career as literary critic.

It was Peadar O'Donnell who first suggested the idea of a magazine to O'Faolain. It was he who found the money and the paper, the first being considerably easier to come by than the second. With shortages so extreme the last thing that industrial companies needed or wanted was advertising. O'Donnell was able with characteristic wryness to reassure them that they need have no fear of increase in demand for their goods as a result of *Bell* advertisements. Actually the normal print for an issue was around three thousand, of which a thousand were bought outside of the country. Leading bene-factors were Joe McGrath, J. P. Digby of Pye Radio and the proprietors of the Kilkenny Woollen Mills. O'Donnell always said that O'Faolain 'gave it stature': under him it would have been, and later perhaps was 'a more rowdy assembly'. At the time both men were in their early forties (O'Faolain barely so) and each was well known as a man-of-letters, but of markedly different careers. O'Faolain had been on De Valera's side in the Civil War but, growing disenchanted, became an academic abroad. He had returned to Ireland in 1932 and had supported himself by his writing which by then included novels, stories, biographies and an Abbey play. He had the customary reward paid by a grateful country: his first collection of stories, *Midsummer Night Madness* (1932) and his novel *Bird Alone* (1936) had been banned. Yet his later harrying of censorship was not personal nor was his impatience with a sentimental view of the Irish language. Both seemed to him stupid and rather dishonest.

O'Donnell had been a teacher and a trade-union organiser before taking part in the Troubles and served two years in prison under the Free State administration. After his escape and amnesty he had continued a career of quasi-revolutionary socialism, defending the Left and organising and agitating on behalf of underprivileged at home and abroad. He had supported the government side in Spain in 1936 and was regarded by the more nervous among the conservative Irish as the socialist devil incarnate. He had also become a very fine writer with four novels (among them the world-famous *Islanders* (1828)) two volumes of autobiography, some political pamphlets and an Abbey play to his credit. This was *Wrack* (1933) doing with rather more social awareness for the fisher-men of North West Donegal what Synge had done for the islanders of Aran. His contributions to O'Faolain's *Bell* and his own editorials continued his political journalism, in his most characteristically abrasive and witty style. He was particularly interested in the Protestants of the North. The pages of *The*

Bell were thrown open to them in a friendly and fearless way. In general *The Bell* reflected the spirit and sometimes opposing views of its two founders and it was the mingling of these antinomies that gave it its special strength and flavour.

The list of associate editors includes such people as Honor Tracy, Val Mulkerns, H. A. L. Craig, and Anthony Cronin. These have all become well-known in other formats; Val Mulkerns and Honor Tracy are writers of novels and short stories, Craig is famous for his radio scripts and Cronin has written a novel, much poetry and is one of Ireland's leading critics. Louis MacNeice acted for a while as poetry editor. The list of contributors reads like a roll-of-honour of Irish literature and there are sufficient contributions from outside Ireland to establish a claim for *The Bell* as a European journal, when most of Europe was in darkness.

Choosing a representative anthology from the archives requires that the editor make a selection from 180 short stories and 250 other items, including poems and general articles. As well there were regular features such as The Bellman interviews and The Open Window and the usual battery of all kinds of reviews. I have tried to make the book characteristic of *The Bell* in its heyday within the limits of topicality and permanent worth. Any imbalance must be ascribed to me. One decision may seem strange: Sean O'Faolain wrote in all twelve stories for the magazine and Frank O'Connor nine, but since they are all in print (and will, I expect, remain so) I have decided to represent the first by some of his editorials and the second by a delightful biographical sketch of George Russell. For the same reasons, I have not included any of Liam O'Flaherty's nine stories and have represented James Plunkett by the one *Bell* story which is not in print.

I would like to take this opportunity of stating my indebtedness to Sean and Eileen O'Faolain, Peadar O'Donnell, David Marcus, Val Mulkerns and many others for their exemplary kindness and help — and to Rudi Holzapfel's *Index of Contributors* without which my work would have been infinitely more tedious.   *Sean McMahon*

THIS IS YOUR MAGAZINE
By SEAN O'FAOLAIN

T HE BELL has, in the usual sense of the word, no policy. We leave it to nature to give the magazine its own time-created character. A boy grows into personality. A man is worth calling a man only in so far as he defines his own character for himself — makes it up out of the gifts of his fathers, the memories of his childhood, the dreams of his boyhood, the ambitions of his youth, the passions of his years, the strength of his own four bones. This magazine will, like-wise, grow into character and meaning. By the time you have read three issues you will be familiar with its character. By the time you have read twelve you will take its character for granted. That would not happen with every magazine, but this is not so much a magazine as a bit of Life itself, and we believe in Life, and leave Life to shape us after her own image and likeness.

That was why we chose the name of 'The Bell'. Any other equally spare and hard and simple word would have done; any word with a minimum of associations. If you begin to think of alternatives you will see why we could not have used *any* of the old symbolic words. They are as dead as Brian Boru, Granuaile, the Shan Van Vocht, Banba, Roisin Dubh, Fodhla, Cathleen ni Houlihan, the swords of light and the risings of the moon. These belong to the time when we growled in defeat and dreamed of the future. That future has arrived and, with its arrival, killed them. All our symbols have to be created afresh, and the only way to create a living symbol is to take a naked thing and clothe it with new life, new association, new meaning, with all the vigour of the life we live in the Here and Now. We refused to use the word Irish, or Ireland, in the title. We said,

'It will plainly be that by being alive.' Our only job was to encourage Life to speak. When she speaks, then *The Bell* will itself become a symbol, and its 'policy' will be self-evident.

All over Ireland — this is the expression of our Faith — there are men and women with things itching them like a grain stuck in a tooth. You who read this know intimately some corner of life that nobody else can know. You and Life have co-operated to make a precious thing which is your secret. You know a turn of the road, an old gateway somewhere, a well-field, a street-corner, a wood, a handful of quiet life, a triangle of sea and rock, something that means Ireland to you. It means the whole world. Men and women who have suffered or died in the name of Ireland, who have thereby died for Life as they know it, have died for some old gateway, some old thistled lag-field in which their hearts have been stuck since they were children. These are the things that come at night to tear at an exile's heart. That is Life. You possess a precious store of it. If you will share it with all of us you will make this bell peal out a living message.

The Bell will ring a note this way and a note that way. The wind will move it and a faint sigh come from the top of the tower. Some passing traveller will finger the rope and send out his cry. Some man who knows how to ring a proper peal will make the clapper shout. People will hear these chance notes to the north and people will hear them to the south, and when they say, in field or pub, in big house or villa house, 'There is the bell,' they will echo the replication of its notes, and the air will carry the echo wider and wider. Each note a message, each echo an answer, each answer a further message — can you not imagine them a linking, widening circle of notes, a very peal of bells, murmuring all over the land?

There is, as I have said, one thing in which you must praise or blame us who are running *The Bell,* and we need both praise and blame in order to know if we are on the right scent. It is our job to have a flair, a nose, a hound's smell for the real thing, for the thing that is alive and kicking, as against the thing that is merely pretending to be alive. We have to go out nosing for bits of individual veracity, hidden in the dust-heaps of con-vention, imitation, timidity, traditionalism, wishful thinking. In that search our only advantage is that of being professional writers, publicists and, after a mild and, we hope, civilised fashion, somewhat unconventional people ourselves. The pro-

fessional writer's job, as for himself (as for others when he
turns critic) is to be able to sense the synthetic thing a mile
away.

You will notice that we do not ask, primarily, for perfection
in the craftwork; we ask, first and before all, for the thing that
lies lurking at the bottom of each man's well, and, if you look
through this first number, you will see several things whose
merit is not chiefly Art but Truth, but which for that are worth
a hundred thousand things that are full of Art but, as for Truth,
are as skinny as Famine. If, then, you are a professional writer
we want your best and only your best. If you doubt whether
you have a gift of the written word, and yet do want to set
down something that is vital to yourself, there is a special
section where you can try your hand.

This Ireland is young and earnest. She knows that somewhere, among the briars and the brambles, there stands the
reality which the generations died to reach – not, you notice,
the Ideal; our generation is too sober to talk much about
Ideals, though we may think of it by any fine name there is,
the Holy Grail, the Sacred Altar, the dream we have called by
those hundred names now gone out of date. We are living
experimentally. Day after day we are all groping for that reality,
and many of our adventures must be a record of error and
defeat. Some of our efforts must equally be steps nearer that
practicable, possible fineness and decency. In recording them
all, the defeats and the victories, the squalors and the enchant-
ments, how can we have any 'policy' other than to stir outselves
to a vivid awareness of what we are doing, what we are becoming, what we are? That is why we say that this is your magazine.
Whether you know it or not, admit it or not, so long as what
you read is true – you wrote it.

The Bell is quite clear about certain practical things and will,
from time to time, deal with them – the Language, Partition,
Education, and so forth. In general *The Bell* stands, in all such
questions, for Life before any abstraction, in whatever
magnificent words it may clothe itself. For we eschew abstractions, and will have nothing to do with generalisations that are
not capable of proof by concrete experience. Generalisation (to
make one) is like prophecy, the most egregious form of error,
and abstractions are the luxury of people who enjoy befuddling
themselves methodically. We prefer, likewise, the positive to

the negative, the creative to the destructive. We ban only lunatics and sour-bellies. We are absolutely inclusive. We take our stand, for that, on the noble words of Alice Stopford Green in presenting the Senate with a casket to hold its Constitution:-

From the beginning, Ireland has been rich in her hospitality to men of goodwill coming within her borders. And at all times there have been incomers who have responded honourably to that generosity and have become faithful members of her people. She has had her rewards among the strangers who, under her wide skies, have felt the wonder of the land, and the quality of its people, and have entered into her commonwealth.

Whoever you are, then, O reader, Gentile or Jew, Protestant or Catholic, priest or layman, Big House or Small House — *The Bell* is yours.

SEAN O'FAOLAIN was born John Whelan in Cork in February, 1900, the son of Denis Whelan, an officer of the Royal Irish Constabulary. He awoke to patriotism in 1916 and for the next eight years was active in the Irish Volunteers, taking the Republican side in the Civil War. Disenchantment followed and he turned to an academic career; after a period of teaching in colleges in the US and Britain he returned to Ireland to live by his pen. Since then he has become in a characteristically self-deprecatory way, Ireland's complete man-of-letters, a latter-day Great Cham of Literature. His best original work is to be found in his stories which for excellence are challenged alone by Frank O'Connor. Eight volumes of these have been published, the most recent in 1978. To this should be added three novels, four biographies, three travel books, two books of literary criticism, a most challenging reappraisal of Irish history, an eminently revivable play, *She Had to do Something* (1937) and an autobiography, *Vive Moi* (1964). Some of his finest contributions to literature were done during the *Bell* period when his editorials rose to the greatest heights of anti-philistine, *pro patria* journalism and his work as editor literally created new Irish writers. He lives in Dun Laoghaire near Dublin.

'This Is Your Magazine' was the first editorial he wrote for *The Bell*. It is typical of his stimulating and sensible approach to the running of a journal in the Ireland of 1940. In it he delineated the spiritual geography of *The Bell* country and indicated what it required from future contributors. It was an offer that many could not refuse.

THIS IS YOUR MAGAZINE   Sean O'Faolain   *October 1940.*

KEDNAMINSHA
By PATRICK KAVANAGH

You wore a heather jumper then,
A hat of clouds and on your feet
Shoes made by craft-gods out of peat.
No poet ever drew a pen
To bind with words wild goats and men
In such a glen. O, Time's deceit
Flirts here in Dublin's Grafton Street.
Yet I recall your quarrymen
Shouting among the granite gables,
Sitting on stone-stools sipping tea.
My eye that scans dull restaurant tables
In the glass of memory plain can see
Great iron men and the loves they seize
And young goats praying on broken knees.

PATRICK KAVANAGH Ireland's best known poet since Yeats was born, as many of his readers will know, in Inishkeen, Co. Monaghan and lived there as shoemaker, farmer, poet and prosewriter till his 'hegira' to Dublin in 1939. His early work *Ploughman* (1936) and his memoir *The Green Fool* (1938) had made his name known as a fine poet and gifted writer but it was not until the publication of his long poem, *The Great Hunger* (1942), which troubled the consciences of the Garda Siochana so much that his reputation became spread abroad. His novel, *Tarry Flynn* (1948) which had strong elements of autobiography in it confirmed his reputation. Excerpts of it had been published earlier in *The Bell.* His poetry changed somewhat after he had settled in Dublin but it remained of a high quality in spite of his troubled and litigious life. He died in 1967.

A.E. – A PORTRAIT
By FRANK O'CONNOR

I MET him first when I was about twenty and working in a Wicklow library. I believe it was shortly after he had published my first poem. I soon got to know that office of his well. It was a top room at the back of an old Georgian house that overlooked a desert of chimney-pots. The brown wall-paper was his own work and decorated with Burne-Jones divinities in gilded dress. He sat at a desk by the upper window, beside a long table of proofs and papers and manuscripts. He bounced up when he saw you. 'Ah, my dear man, come in.' He was the friend of every young writer. He read our manuscripts, printed us, found us publishers, supervised our reading. He even wanted to arrange our marriages. At least he wanted to arrange mine. Finally he succeeded in getting us together at dinner, myself and the firl he wanted me to marry. 'Isn't he nice?' he asked the girl. 'Isn't she nice?' he asked me.

He was a big man; burly, clumsy, untidy, with wild hair and long brown beard; tufted eyebrows, and a broad, soft, red face with high cheekbones that was very like the famous bust of Socrates. Under the tobacco-stained flow of the beard, his lips were soft and his teeth in a bad state. Usually he sat well back in his chair, rather heavily because of his fat, beaming benevolently through his spectacles, his pipe between his teeth, his legs crossed, his socks hanging down. Sometimes in earnest mood, he leaned forward with his two fat hands on his knees. He had a trick of suddenly lowering his head as though about to butt, and looking at you over the spectacles, which impressed you by a certain penetrating, almost elfin quality, a daft, glittering, inconsequential brightness.

He was an extraordinarily fidgety, restless man, forever jumping up to find some poem he was about to print (of course it was lost in the heap of manuscripts) or some book he was reviewing. As he was very short-sighted, he held them very close to his eyes, and his head skipped from side to side as he followed the lines. In his excitement he dropped whole chunks of sentences, interrupted a sentence with an explosion of laughter or an eager, boyish 'Isn't that good? Isn't that clever?'

On Sunday evenings I went regularly to Rathgar, and grew accustomed to the deep peal of the bell, the yelp of the old dog and the hasty handclasp that pulled you in. He had a double room, lined to the ceiling with his own paintings: landscapes with dancing figures in the manner of Corot, figure paintings of spirits in boats or naked on hilltops against yellow spirit rays. The tea things were laid in a corner. It was a typical suburban room, except for the pictures and the terra cotta figurines on the mantelpiece. There was an upholstered settle at either side of the fire, an old sofa in the middle of the room and a comfortable armchair from which he presided. The unshaded lights beat down on those rows of crudely coloured canvases with their bright greens and blues, and except for some sort of bust of himself as a young man and a Jack Yeats drawing, there is nothing I remember with pleasure. He answered the door himself, and for the first hour sat intent, jumping up at an imaginary knock, a little flushed and flurried, running his hands through his hair and beard as he strode to the door. It was only about midnight when casual visitors had gone and only a few intimate friends remained that the night really began to be interesting. Then he would sigh, ruffle his hair and beard and settle himself in for a chat, leaning back in his armchair, laughing in his throat with his face upturned to the ceiling, listening gravely with lowered head while he twined his beard about his hands. That is how I like to remember that room, when a wind was blowing up Rathgar, and you felt its brightness, its intense friendliness.

Every week he came to my lodgings or flat, on the same evening and at the same hour. He was a creature of habit, the sort of man who all his life will sit at the same table of the same restaurant, and is ill at ease when waited on by any but the waitress he knows. Every evening he said the same thing. 'My dear fellow, I hope I'm not interrupting you.' Then he threw his hat and coat impatiently on the settee (once when I removed them to the hall he looked at me reproachfully and asked 'Was that necessary?') tossed his hair and beard, and settled into his old chair with an expectant beam in his eye. He took a cup of tea, clutching the cup and saucer close to his beard, refused a second cup, always in the same dim, hasty way: 'No, thank you, my dear fellow,' while he looked at you unseeingly over his spectacles, at twenty minutes to eleven glanced at his watch and gasped 'I must be going,' leaped up as though on wires and fumbled rapidly downstairs for the last tram. He always stood almost on the track, signalling wildly with both arms to the driver, and then, without a backward glance, bundled himself on and was half way up the stairs before the tram started.

Any break in the habitual round caused a minor convulsion. He was left with an evening on his hands, and everything had to be readjusted. For weeks after I wouldn't see him. Then one night came the usual impatient knock, and I found him tranquilly waiting on the doorstep stroking his brown beard, his big eyes gleaming behind the spectacles, and as he strode impetuously in, he said in that soft voice of his 'My dear fellow, I hope I'm not interrupting you.'

He liked fixed days for doing fixed things; fixed ways of doing them. One evening, without even waiting for an opening, he greeted me with 'I was in Howth yesterday. Hadn't been there for twelve years.' It was his day for visiting an old friend, X, with whom he had quarrelled. Next week, well on in the night, he said casually 'I was at X's yesterday.'

He was a creature of habit, and his conversation, like his life, ran in patterns: well-formed phrases, ideas, quotations and anecdotes which he repeated over a lifetime without altering an inflection. He was not very skilful in their use; the patchwork was obvious, and after a time you could see the subject coming from a long way off. It was curious, that repetitiousness, for he was a man of intense intellectual vitality: ideas came to him almost too readily, and his experience, when he chose to draw on it, was profound and varied — particularly when it was remembered casually, as a result of something said, and came to him with the freshness and excitement of a thing recovered.

'A.E.,' I once teased him, 'Joyce makes you say "The only thing that matters about a work of art is out of how deep a life does it spring." '

'Well, that's clever of him,' A.E. exclaimed with genuine surprise, looking at me earnestly over his spectacles.

'That's true, you know. I may quite well have said that.'

He said it at least once a day. He also said that one must wait patiently at home and let experience come, as it would, all Nature thought good for one to have. He had never sought for anything. It had all come to him. That might be called the doctrine of psychic attraction. Allied to this was the doctrine of the diversity of inner and outer. It was dangerous to try and get rid of whatever afflicted you because it might be this tension that made you what you were. These were patterns of speech that seemed to have lasted him a lifetime. As well as those 'great thoughts,' which, after you had heard them a few times ceased to be great thoughts ('You cannot stand forever on tiptoe' or 'you cannot deepen a superficies'); he had by heart a number of poems and prose passages that had excited him as a boy. His memory was amazing, but these, too, had become so much a matter of habit that he seemed to have lost the power of criticising them.

His own poems, as often as he repeated them – and he did it pretty often – never changed a comma, as though they had been immortalised in the form in which he had written them thirty or forty years before – he used to boast that he knew by heart every line of verse he had written. I couldn't understand this, for he was certainly the first who pointed out to me that language is finite, and that the beauty of verse wears itself away by repetition. But Yeats' early work as well, for all his labours on improving it, never altered on A.E.'s lips. He remembered the poems word for word as they had been written or as Yeats had recited them to him, and I think he resented the changes. If he is 'the old school friend' Yeats supposed to have liked them 'because they reminded him of his own youth' that is too simple a reading of the story. A.E. was too fine a literary critic not to know that Yeats' changes were improvements, but in some extraordinary way, that habit-forming complex, like a hardening of the arteries, would not permit him to see Yeats' work with the same clear eyes with which he saw Higgins' or Kavanagh's or mine – and though A.E. was very good, very kind, very flattering, he was a man you couldn't take in.

But those early poems of Yeats had become so much a part of his mental make-up that he could not bear to see them altered or slighted. As though it troubled his conscience, he would praise the artistry of the later Yeats, but it always ended up in the same way, and in a think slight, high-pitched, slow, monotonous croon, shaking his shaggy head, his eyes glazed with rapture, he began to say 'The Indian On God.'

As I grew to know him better, I noticed more and more that oscillation between admiration and dislike of the later Yeats, at times it almost unbalanced him; and I am convinced that habit had gone so far with him that till the day of his death he saw in Yeats only the boy he had once known, who 'used to rush into his bedroom at three or four in the morning to say a new poem for him,' the boy who wore a beard, 'and never again looked as noble as he did with the beard.' How subtly, how heart-breakingly provincial is that touch! One can almost hear the voice of the local intellectual leaning over the town bridge at midnight. 'Of course, I don't think he ever again did anything as good as a little one-act comedy he wrote while he was here.'

I am certain that charming boy and his lovely lyrics were always for Russell the real Yeats, and that whenever he went to see Yeats it was in hope of finding some trace of him again, and that those violent oscillations of emotion in which he raged at the later Yeats and his work, were the result of despair at finding again only the changeling Yeats; the detached and mannered public man who talked in difficult images as though from an Olympian height. He still called him 'Willie Yeets' as he must have done when a boy, and there is a certain significance in the trick.

He talked a lot about growing old, and about 'the fog in his brain,' and that from the first days I knew him. This was usually a prelude to a holiday, 'to restore my fading wits,' a painting, poetry-writing holiday which was his only escape from his regime of habit, but every year he went to the same place in Donegal, to the same house, I believe, painted exactly the same sort of pictures, wrote the same sort of poems, corresponded regularly with his friends, inviting them to join him, and scribbling the same 'view from my window' so that one holiday was much like the next except for whatever book he brought to read in the intervals of shockers.

That habit-forming complex was all over his conversation, his prose, his verse, his painting. Critics accused him of vagueness and platitude, sometimes very bitterly, and it was hard to

defend him, but for myself I feel certain that those vicious
tricks of style which obscure a really individual perception in
language where repetition has killed all sense of wonder are
nothing more or less than bad habits picked up heaven knows
how or where in boyhood. At the first page of the first prose
book of his I open I find two clichés – 'the genie in the innermost' and 'an outcast from the light,' and these bring back
others with which his letters to me are filled, 'deep own being'
and 'pleroma' and 'the Dark Fortnight' – all clichés. But there
was nothing of the charlatan about Russell. The clichés are not
intended to blind the reader; they mean nothing; for thirty or
forty years they had meant nothing to him; he had probably
heard them at an age when we are impressed by such phrases,
and gone on using them, unaware of the effect they produced
on others. The repetition of them over a hundred or more pages
stuns and stupefies the reader and makes him think not of a
universe of spiritual essences, but a universe of cotton wool,
yet that book, *Song and its Fountains,* contains the finest
criticism of Yeats ever written.

Is it the same with his poems. Some Japanese artist described
himself as 'The Old Man Mad about Painting,' but A.E. was the
Old Man Mad About Poetry, and Heaven knows from what
early saturation in Non-conformist hymns a man so quick to the
magic of verse picked up those barbarous, jangling rhythms;
the metrical equivalent of clichés, though there are clichés
enough.

"And the heaven of heavens departed and the visions passed away
With the seraph of the darkness martyred in the fires of day."

A friend of his who understands painting ascribed the quality
of his pictures to bad sight, but surely those children who made
their way into the austerest landscapes to the exclusion of every
other form of created life were clichés; so much a trick of pencil
or brush that I used to see him idly scribbling them, as another
might scribble his name, over notebooks, sketchbooks and
presentation copies. Surely, he had met them first in those
misty landscapes of Corot? Poems, pictures, philosophy,
conversation – politics and economics, too, I suspect – all were
memories of memories of memories, all connection with the
real world broken, generalised into nothingness and produced

gaily and inconsequentially, without tension or anguish.

Once he painted a beautiful little picture as a present for myself or another friend, and, admiring it, I asked what the tree in the foreground was. I had no intention of being impertinent, but he did not like the question and drew into himself. 'Oh,' he said shortly, with that wooden face he put on when he was hurt, 'a tree, just a tree.' Then in that light, mocking mood in which I liked him best he quoted a story of some Scotch painter. 'When I draw a picture of a woman, I draw a thick, black line. I grant you it's no' in the least like a woman, but it's my idea of a woman, and Bergson says it's the idea of a thing that matters.'

With him it was always the idea of a thing that mattered. The friend of whom I have spoken also pointed out that never in Russell's pictures is there a thing made by human agency; a house or tool or vehicle. And it is equally strange that I cannot remember such a thing as an individual tree; oak or beech or ash. Nothing but 'a thick black line!'

He produced abundantly, effortlessly, yet seemed to find no real delight in his work, because picture, essay, poem, created without the anguish of the artist, left an unsatisfied creative urge, and he can never have known the utter emptiness of the writer who exhausts himself in one supreme effort and feels there can be nothing left to say. The poets he praised most frequently to me were Shakespeare and Byron, and these because each had expressed his whole moral being in verse. He enthused in the same way about the abundance of Tolstoy, the overflowing of the great crater, and Dumas was his favourite among novelists. He used to quote with glee that duel scene when one of the Musketeers, eyeing his opponent, says, 'I perceive, if we do not kill one another, we shall become very good friends.' But perhaps I am exaggerating this side of his character, because once, when he found me in an empty mood he chuckled and said 'You know what the hens say when they've laid an egg. "Oh, God, God, God, there are going to be no more eggs." That's what it means.'

I liked him best when he was gay and teasing and sly, as then, or even, in his innocent way, malicious, or, as happened once or twice when people were stupid, downright rude; because at such times he had to improvise, he burst into sudden fantasies, and then something of the wilful, wicked, unfed, sleeping artist temperament came out.

That is how I like to remember him: light, quick, gay and spontaneous, with just a little savour of malice. I like to remember him when he really laughed and shook in all his fat, and his soft voice disappeared down his throat. Then it seemed to me there was a real incandescence in him. I liked him less when he was benevolent and didn't like him at all when he was philosophic.

It is easier for me now to see why. The picture of him as the good grey poet is all nonsense; that was simply a cold crust of habit about an interior volcano, and it was the volcano I loved. Sometimes you saw it in his eyes when he looked into the fire, sometimes in the wooden face he put on when wounded, some-times in one brief sentence with a dull reverberation in it that suggested a life-time of suppression and reserve. Now, I think him a morbidly sensitive man of ungovernable passions, and perhaps with some secret grief. But the gaiety in which his spirit released itself does not appear at all in his work, and because an artist's temperament is a wild beast and must be fed on raw meat, somebody in a hundred years' time will wonder why we thought him a great man.

FRANK O'CONNOR was born Michael O'Donovan in Cork in 1903 and is famous throughout the world for his short stories several of which may claim their places in any world anthology of the *genre*. His literary career included services on the board of the Abbey Theatre, the writing of two plays, two novels, some stirring, if idiosyncratic criticism including a study of the short story, his own form, so to speak, *The Lonely Voice* (1963), the interpretation of old Gaelic literature for modern readers in superb translations especially *Kings Lords and Commons* (1961), *The Midnight Court* (1959) and *The Backward Look* (1967). Apart from writing many stories and essays for *The Bell* he also ran the feature 'The Belfry' in 1940 and 1941, did some of the profiles for 'The Bellman' and wrote anonymously the pieces 'Orphans' (October, November 1940) which he afterwards incorporated in his first volume of autobiography *An Only Child* (1961). His portrait of AE is typical of his compelling narrative ability and of the rich style of his prose. He died in 1966.

AE A PORTRAIT   Frank O'Connor   *November 1940*

TWENTY-FIVES

By MICHAEL J. MURPHY

F LIP-flip-flip–Slap! He turns up an Ace.
'Rob an' play an' sport your Ace,' mumbles a grizzled old man absently as if saying an adage; but he is concentrating on his hand of cards. Every player is scanning his hand. There are six players around the uncovered table of pock-drilled plain boards. Timid youths with the lips and complexions of schoolgirls shoulder old men whose tanned jaws are lined like Morocco leather. Veterans and greenhorns.

The greenhorns use the slang of the game self-consciously; but the slang of the game holds much of the atmosphere and appeal which gathers about a 'board' of seasoned players. Laconic speech suggests agile minds. The greenhorns dream of such an attainment. The banshee wind coming through the keyhole stops, and the smoky lamp ceases to jump. The dog on the hearth growls in his dreams, stretches, and amuses the stoical-faced cat.

'What's thrump?' The speaker is almost grim-looking, almost suspicious, too. An old fellow flicks a furtive glance at that expression and purses his lips.

'What's thrump?' another voice asks as if coming from distant dreams quite suddenly.

'Look,' snaps a veteran, swaying backwards and spitting sarcastically on to the earthen floor.

Two other pair of eyes flick alert, appraising glances at him. His remark has set their calculative minds in motion, hazarding a guess as to the possible strength of the hand which inspired the disgruntled word. One can hear the fire flickering. An old fellow chews black-plug tobacco with the lazy grind of a cow enjoying her cud. Now and then he flicks a glance at the card on

top of the pack out of play. Some one clears his throat huskily
'Rob.... someone. Who dealt?'
'Hearts thrump! Rob will yeh?' Irritably.
'How's the play?'
Heads lift from the cards. The greenhorns rest their elbows on the table, kissing their cards. An old fellow switches quick side glances at a greenhorn's hand, then at his own, thinking, pitting cards against other possible hands.
'Hold down yer hand,' an advice drawls.
'First trick five an' no man ten! Rob!'
'Don't be all night, man!'
The dealer is a young fellow, and he robs. The play begins. A silence spreads itself, marked by the clack of spittle; the swift intake of air through nostrils; a quietly-cleared throat. Suspense settles over the board.
The cards still flick. No one speaks. Brows come down suddenly, screening perplexed eyes, others lift easily. Rows of skin corrugations furrow young foreheads. This is furtively observed by the veterans, who purse their lips again with sarcasm equally furtive. A hopeful gleam starts in a pair of eyes, and burns down again. An old fellow has stopped chewing as a card is played; he swells his cheeks, sighs down his nose, and begins chewing again. Every time a greenhorn plays a card the others seem to stop breathing.
So far, play has been routine; but drama slips into the atmosphere; there is a threat in the air. The greenhorn is playing again, the greenest greenhorn with the cap sideways on his head, with a reckless light in his eyes, and his open mouth resembling a kettle spout. The old fellow tries to spit while still watching the youth. Innocently, the young fellow looks at them in turn, appealingly.
'Play will yeh?' the old boy snaps, spitting quickly.
'Ah....!' Down comes that card. The tension has been tautened as he started to speak. The vets rise from their seats, their faces grim. He has played a Knave on an idle man's tentative thrust for a first trick. The tension snaps. They all seem to be shouting at once. A minor uproar. The room seems to rock.
'Sufferin' ...'
'What the...!'
'Ye lug yeh!'

The firest from their eyes mix, and seem to ignite the deep blush on the face of the youth, who struggles with his cap, fidgeting, dropping his eyes.

'Why the divil didn't yeh hold yer Knave an' not beat an idle man? An' yeh saw him rob the head deck of the Ace. Didn't I tell yeh afore — Show us your hand,' he demands with sudden truculence. The greenhorn obeys docilely. The old men all roar at once.

'An' the Fingers in your hand! An' yeh bate an' idle man!'

'An' let a robbin' man rise Ten.'

'Is that keepin' in the play?'

In relays they tirade him, enjoying his squirming. He smiles embarrassedly. The other greenhorn blushes, too, as if some of the abuse affected himself. For, it is a tradition of the game that selfish, self-centred aims should be suppressed, with potential and dramatically belated swoops to snap up tricks also, in order to keep the result in abeyance for another hand. At a board one night no man was 'Twenty Five,' and the fifth hand being dealt! It made a legend.

And greenhorns take it, unaware that it is an epitome of life itself, dreaming of a day when they shall sit at boards with the old hands, arguing points of play with them, recalling played tricks as if the facts of them had been as indented on memory as a tune on a record.

'That's Twenty Fives. The game of every card-player and rustic, but despised by the gambler. The stakes are a half-penny. You can be 'broke', and still be thrilled over it.

MICHAEL J. MURPHY was born in Liverpool in 1913 to parents who sprang from South Armagh farming stock, though his father was a seaman. The boy was brought back to South Armagh and received his formal and informal education around Dromintee that magical country which figures so largely in his work. After leaving school at fourteen he worked for local farmers all the while assimilating the great store of Ulster folklife for which he is famous. He began freelance writing and broadcasting in his twenties and was invited to join the Irish Folklore Commission which is now a department of UCD and to which he is still attached. He has written many stories and has had plays produced in the Abbey (Dublin), the Group (Belfast) and the Arts (London). His first collection, *At Slieve*

Gullion's Foot was published in 1940 and his most recent *Mountainy Crack* published by Blackstaff Press in 1977 contains the piece printed here. His latest appearance in print was in Berlin with *Sinn und Form.* He is married with four children and lives still in Dromintee on the Armagh side of Newry.

TWENTY-FIVES   Michael J. Murphy   *December 1940*

CEILIDHE

By W. R. ROGERS

So they went, leaving a picnic-litter of talk
And broken glitter of jokes, the burst bags of spite:
In comes Contempt the caretaker, eye on ceiling,
Broom in armpit, and with one wide careless cast
Sweeps the stuttering rubbish out of memory,
Opens the shutters, puts out the intimate lamp,
And, a moment, gazes on the mute enormities
Of distant dawn. And far doors bang in mind, idly.

WILLIAM ROBERT RODGERS, known universally as 'Bertie', even, one suspects, to his congregation was that rare but not extinct species a Northern nationalist Presbyterian clergyman. Born in Belfast in 1909 he experienced the misery of the sectarian violence of the Twenties but rejected the polarisation that followed it. He ministered in Loughgall, Co. Armagh from 1934 to 1946 and afterwards became a BBC producer. He compiled a number of Irish Literary Portraits for the Third Programme which have become classics of radio. He was elected to the Irish Academy of Letters in 1951 because of the excellence of his poetry. He was a close friend of Louis MacNeice but their often discussed book on Ireland never materialised. His poetry is collected in two volumes: *Awake* (1941) and *Europa and the Bull* (1952). He died in the United States in 1969.

CEILIDHE   W. R. Rodgers   *February 1941*

THE TAILOR'S 'BUSHT'

By ERIC CROSS

I felt that strongly the time the Tailor's 'busht' was being made. For among the Tailor's many friends is Seamus Murphy, the sculptor, and when he proposed making this bust, the Tailor agreed on the spot.

'Damn it man, it was ever said that two heads are better than one and the one I have now I have had for seventy-five years and it is getting the worse for wear. Of course I'll have a new one!'

All the apparatus and materials were assembled and the Tailor inspected them with the interest of a fellow craftsman. Ansty ignored the business in the beginning. Her only interest in it was her resentment of the invasion of the 'Room' – 'with all the ould clay and mortar to make a new divil' – and making fresh disorder of her disorder. The 'Room' at last justified the Tailor's name for and did become for a while what he calls it– 'The Studio'. For an hour or so each day he posed and talked and commented. The measurements interested him and he linked this part of the business with his own craft.

'Many's the time that I have measured a man's body for a new suit of clothes but I never thought that the day would come when I would be measured myself for a new head.'

'I think that we will have a rest for awhile,' suggested Seamus during one session.

'The divil a rest do I need. Do you know that I feel it less than I did the time the whole of my body was making before I was born. There is a considerable improvement in this method. A man can smoke and take his ease and chat away for himself.

The news soon spread that the Tailor's 'image' was being made. Even The Sheep, on his weekly visit mentioned it.

'I did hear tell, Tailor, that you are in the way of having your "image" made. I don't know. But I *did* hear tell.'

'Faith, I am,' agreed the Tailor, 'and a good strong one too. It is going to be made in bronze — the hardest metal that ever was. It was the metal that the Tuathaa de Danaans brought to Ireland with them and it will last for hundreds of years.'

'Indeed!' exclaimed The Sheep, settling down a little further on his stick. 'Tell me, Tailor,' he asked, with a show of interest, 'how will that be done?'

'Yerra, man alive. It's easy enough. You stick your head into a pot of stirabout and when it is cold you pull out your head and melt the metal and pour it into the hole your head made. Then you eat up the stirabout and you find your new head inside the pot.'

'Indeed!' grunted The Sheep. 'Indeed, that's wonderful enough.' The Sheep settled a little more securely on his stick to absorb and digest this new information. After a while he came out of his shell again. 'They tell me that it is unlucky for a man to have his image made, Tailor. Would this be like a photograph, now, could you tell me?'

The Sheep had always refused to stand for his photo.

'Th'anam o'n diabhal! Unlucky! It isn't half so unlucky as going to bed. Many a man had twins as the result of going to bed and, anyway, most people die in bed. If they had real sense they would keep out of bed and then the death would not catch them so easily.'

'Yes. Yes. I suppose that is true,' unreadily assented The Sheep and left very shortly after in case the Tailor might add another to his already great load of fears.

Ansty's interest was awakened when the clay began to take form. Then she was, in the beginning, afraid of it. She removed her cream pans from the Room to a cupboard under the stairs. Whatever curse may fall upon the place as the result of this latest prank of 'himself' the cream must be preserved from harm at all costs. But in spite of her fear, she could not resist a sally. From the safe distance of the doorway she watched the operation once or twice.

'Look at my divil! You'd think to look at him and the mug of him that he was a statoo in a chapel.'

Familiarity with the sight of the 'image' gradually made her contemptuous. But Old Moore did not like the idea at all. In the beginning it was mysterious to him and he could not understand it. When the image was taking form it roused all Old Moore's religious scruples.

'It isn't right, Tailor. It isn't right, I tell you. It's a graven image and it is against the commandments. The church is against it and all the popes.'

'Yerra, what harm! What harm can there be in a head? Didn't you make a couple of small lads, whole and entire, body, head, legs and all, with Nora, and you talk about an old head.'

Then 'Bydam Tighe' came in and he almost scratched his own head off in puzzlement at it. He could not understand it all.

'Bydam, Tailor, I hear that you are having a new head made.'

'That's true enough, Tighe. A brand new head that will last a hundred years, made of bronze, the hardest substance there is. It won't be affected by the heat or the cold or the sun or the rain.'

'Bydam, that's queer. I never heard of that before.'

'It's a new patent, Tighe. They have got a new method of making people because the young people nowadays are failing at the job and the population of the country is going down.'

'Bydam, I didn't hear that.'

'There are a lot of new wonders in the world nowadays, Tighe. There's aeroplanes and cars and wireless and now this new way of making people.'

'Bydam, I have heard it said that wonders will never cease.'

'True for you, Tighe. Wonders will never cease so long as women kiss donkeys.'

Tighe disappeared to brush the road for a while. Then he came back to redden his pipe and to have another look at the Tailor's own head. He did not know that the 'image' was in the other room.

'Bydam, I was thinking, Tailor, will you be able to use it? Will you be able to talk and smoke and see with it?'

'Th'anam o'n diabhal! What the hell do you think that I am having it made for? Do you think that I want to become a dummy? I tell you that when I have this head I will be a different man. You have often heard tell that you can't put a young head on old shoulders. Well, this is what it is. I was thinking of having it the other way at first. Having a new body fitted to my old head. But the expense for the bronze was too much so I am starting with the head first. Then the new brains

would not be so good as the old ones I thought. But then I
thought that the old ones had done a power of thinking in their
time and it would be better after all to start with the head.'

Tighe was lost in wonderment for a while.

'Bydam, Seamus Murphy must be a clever man.'

'Clever! I should think he is. He's as good as Daniel O'Connell
and Owen Roe put together. They were good enough in the old
fashioned way but before he's finished with this business he'll
have the whole of Ireland populated again. It is a much quicker
way than the way you had of going about the business, Tighe.'

'Bydam, it must be. I must talk to herself about it to-night,'
and Tighe went back to 'the most useless bloody job in the
whole world,' in the Tailor's opinion, brushing the road.

The daily sessions continued with interest and much verbal
assistance from the Tailor. He remembered a story about a man
who made a statue — but the story will not bear repetition.

'I think that if you tighten your mouth it would be better,
Tailor,' suggested Seamus.

'True for you, Seamus. It is the loose tongue that does all
the harm in the world. I remember a man by the name of ———'
and it was a quarter of an hour before he stopped talking and
the mouth was tight enough for the work to proceed.

He has one tooth left in his head. It is a very large canine
which is completely useless but of which he is very proud. It
even has a name. He has referred to it always as 'The Inchcape
Rock'.

'I tell you that that tooth has enjoyed itself. It was no fun
in its day when it had all its companions. They were the boys
for you. Many's the half gallon of porter that has swirled
around that, and many is the pig that it has made mincemeat
of.'

'I am going to tackle your hair now, Tailor.'

'Fire away, Seamus, my boy. Fire away. I have forgotten
how many there are of them, but they are all numbered,
according to 'the Book'. But one wrong here or there won't
make any difference. The divil a bit.'

Now and again Ansty peered into the room to see what
progress was being made.

'Will you look at my ould shtal? Will you look at the puss
on him? You'd think that he was all cream, sitting up there
looking like a statoo in the chapel and divil doing nothing all

the time but planning his lies and shtories.'

'You'd better get yourself tidied up a bit,' commanded the Tailor in the midst of one of her commentaries.

'Whyfore should I get tidied?' she asked with surprise.

'We'll have to go and see the priest when this is done.'

'For what, you divil?'

'Th'anam o'n diabhal! Don't be asking questions but do as you are told. We will have to go and get married again. You were only married to the old head and you will have to be married to the new head now or we will be living in sin.'

'Hould, you divil!'

The day for the plaster-casting arrived. The Tailor discovered all manner of possibly useful things for the job in Cornucopia — the butter-box he sits on. When at last the job was done he complimented Seamus. 'A damn neat job. It could not have been done better if I had done it myself.' The cast was trimmed and carried away for the metal casting. Then Seamus brought it back to Garrynapeaka and the whole valley was invited to the exhibition of 'The Tailor's New Skull'. It was placed on the stand in the dim light of the Studio with a dark cloth behind it. The door was closed. The guests were assembled. The stout and the beer and the whiskey were opened and all was expectancy. The occasion was graced by the presence of His Reverence — 'The Saint' — another old friend of the Tailor's, whom Ansty calls 'the biggest divil in Ireland after himself,' with a complete lack of reverence for the cloth. The Saint made a speech on the marvels of this new wonder and opened the Studio door with a string, revealing 'The Tailor's New Skull'.

There was the rapt silence of wonder for a moment. Then Ansty, who was bored with the whole affair and what seemed to her to be a quite unnecessary amount of fuss about nothing at all and who had bustled and pushed through the crowd ripped the silence asunder:

'How are the hens by ye, Johnny Mac?'

Ansty's inconsequential remark brought the assembly back to earth. The Sheep had been gazing, with eyes agog, first at the Tailor and then at the image, scarcely able to believe what he saw. 'It's devilish. It's devilish, I tell you, Tailor.' He grunted assent with his own remark and hastened away from the house with his drink only half finished. Tighe was stirred to expression.

'Bydam!' he gasped, 'Bydam, but... do you know... but it

greatly resembles the Tailor!' The Tailor himself hopped up to it and gave it a crack with his knuckles. 'There you are. A fine head. There's a head will wear out several bodies and it will break the jaws of any flea or midge that tries to bite it!'

'Look at him, will you? Look at my ould shtal,' breaks in Ansty, seeing a chance of pricking the Tailor's latest balloon, 'my ould devil of the two heads and the one he has already is no use by him. It's another bottom he needs for the one he has he's nearly worn out, sitting on it in the corner all day long, and shmoking and planning lies.'

'Wouldn't you like a bust of yourself done, Mrs. Buckley?' asks the Saint, sweetly, almost certain of the reply.

'Busht! Busht!' Ansty snorts with contempt. 'If you want a match for that ould devil you can make a busht of my backside!'

'And to think that Seamus made a busht of that ould devil as though he was a saint in a church. The man must be half cracked. As cracked as himself. Glory be! and to think that he wouldn't settle the leak in the chimney for me! And he with the good mortar and plaster, making a *"busht"*!'

ERIC CROSS was born in Newry, Co. Down of an English father and an Irish mother. By profession a research chemist his claim to fame is as the Boswell of Tim Buckley, the Inchigeela tailor, and of his eloquent wife Ansty. His book *The Tailor and Ansty* contains 'the echo of their innocent laughter', to quote another good friend, Frank O'Connor. The book was banned, of course, but its banning exposed the Irish Censorship Board to a ridicule that even its smug righteousness could not withstand. The book was unbanned again but by this time the old couple were dead, their last years having been made miserable by characteristic merciless clerical bullying. The piece describes the time the Cork sculptor, Seamus Murphy, a regular visitor at the Buckley's cottage, decided to make a bust of the Tailor. Cross lives now in County Mayo. A new collection of short stories, *Silence is Golden,* was published in 1978.

THE TAILOR'S 'BUSHT'   *Eric Cross*   *February 1941*

THE DANCE HALLS

By FLANN O'BRIEN

'JAZZ-HALL' dancing may appear to be a harmless enough business, however unimaginative. Many of our clergy do not think it is and several of the Solomons of the district court are quite certain that it isn't. The dance hall was unknown before the last war and the prevalence of the craze to-day may be taken to be a symptom of a general social change that is bound up with altering conditions of living and working. To-day there are roughly 1,200 licensed halls in the 26 Counties, accounting for perhaps 5,000 dances in a year. Golf and tennis clubs, Volunteer halls and the like do not require a licence. In all, it is a fair guess that 10,000 dances are held in a year, an average of three a day. In terms of time, this means that there is a foxtrot in progress in some corner of Erin's isle throughout the whole of every night and day. This is hard going for a small country. Is it appalling? Is it true that the rural dance hall is a place to be avoided by our sisters? Is it fair to say that Ireland is peopled by decadent alcoholics in pumps?

In 1935 the Public Dance Halls Act was passed. It was designed to control dancing — by then a vast industry and a country-wide neurosis — and to wipe out abuses bearing on everything from sanitation to immorality. The problem itself and the operation of the Act have occupied pages of news-paper space since. Bishops and judges have made strong comments. Satan has been blamed personally. There is, however, no great uniformity in outlook or conclusion. Here are some reported pronouncements, picked more or less at random. Probably very few of the pronouncers have ever paid fourpence to swelter for four hours in an insanitary shack.

Some time ago the evil of commercialised dance halls was so great that the Government felt bound to legislate. This legislation has been a dismal farce. It is the opinion of many that it has done more harm than good. — *Most Rev. Dr. Gilmartin.*

The Act was the most excellent passed since 1922. It only required a very modest quota of sweet reasonableness and goodwill to work it.
— *District Justice Johnson.*

The provisions of the Public Dance Halls Act, 1935, were unworkable and had been recognised by the Bench as unworkable.   — *District Justice Little.*

There is one agency which Satan has set up here and there in recent years that does incalculably more harm than all the others we have mentioned. It deserves to be called after his name, for he seems to preside at some of the dark rites enacted there. We have in mind the rural dance hall, owned by a private individual, run for profit, open to all who pay, without any exception of persons, conducted with no sort of responsible supervision. — *Most Rev. Dr. Morrisroe.*

He saw no harm in a well-conducted dance. It was his wish that people in Raphoe Diocese should get as much innocent recreation as possible and make the most of their opportunities. For that reason he was very pleased to see such a fine new hall being provided in Letterkenny. — *Most Rev.* Dr. *MacNeely.*

They were disposed to think that if the dance finished at midnight on a fine night, people would not be inclined to go home but would walk around the country. — *Solicitor Lisdoonvarna Court.*

All-night dancing should be abolished completely. No licence should be granted to a hall which is contiguous to or within easy distance of a public house.* — *Rev. R. S. Devane, S.J.*

In order to satisfy himself as to the suitability of a place proposed for public dancing, he would require that elevations and sections of the premises, accompanied by a block plan showing the position in relation to adjacent buildings, be lodged with the chief clerk of the court, and that certified copies be supplied to the Superintendent of the division concerned. — *District Justice Little.*

The Galway Hospital Committee have passed a resolution drawing attention to the prevalence of sexual immorality as shown by the number of illegitimate births in the Galway Maternity Hospital and stating that it deplores this departure from the Gaelic tradition of purity, caused, in their opinion, by the lessening of parental control and want of supervision at dances and other amusements. — *'Irish Independent'.*

I am in position to state that the vast majority of unmarried mothers have met with downfall under circumstances remote from dance halls or dances. — *Dr. J. F. O'Connor, Macroom.*

Illegitimate births in the 26 counties, 1929: 1,853; 1939: 1,781. — *Returns of the Registrar-General.*

Father Devane is anxious to know how far dance halls set up a restlessness that causes girls to emigrate. He wonders, too, how far dance halls lessen 'the strenuous efforts so vitally necessary in the present agricultural crisis.' He asks why there are so many dance halls in Donegal. You follow Father Devane with your coat off. You ask no questions. You tie up dance halls and emigration and make the dance hall nearly as all-embracing a source of evil as the British connection, and hint darkly. ... There is a background to the dance hall. Take Donegal, the black spot. Social life in the crowded areas there is a grand affair. Dancing played its part. During the winter there were endless excuses for raffles — a dance till midnight at 3d. a head. The schoolhouse was used for big nights. The parochial hall was there, but there was always too much style — and the charge was high 'to keep out the rough'. The raffle and the schoolhouse are no more. The parochial hall is still a pain in the neck. So the local dance hall arises. It does not come in. It grows. Nothing so natural to these areas is bad. To be sure, 'nothing human is perfect'. The men who built these halls are just neighbours to the boys and girls who attend them. The girls don't emigrate in search of dancing or glitter, but in search of wages. Many Donegal girls come to Dublin. Some get quite good wages. But they don't stay in Dublin, although Dublin has dance halls galore. They feel lonely in Dublin, so they go to Glasgow where hundreds of neighbours have made their homes... – *Peadar O'Donnell in a letter to the 'Irish Press'.*

An application on behalf of Rev. Fr. Monaghan, C.C., Killanny, was made for extension of a licence for dances at a carnival.

Justice Goff – 'This is a marquee. I am afraid I cannot. – *'Irish Independent'.*

When District Justice Walsh was told that a dance licence for a Milford hall was lapsing as the hall was being converted into a cinema, he said: 'That is worse. At least the dancing money is kept in the country.' – *'Irish Independent'.*

* But is there any such spot in all Ireland?

Let us visit some of these 'vestibules of hell'. If you want to go to a dance in the country, you buy a copy of the local paper and turn to the dance page. This, so to speak, is the countryman's leader page. Only after reading every word of it does he penetrate to the coursing notes and after that a long time may elapse before he reaches the customary holocaust involving those 10,000 Chinese coolies.

Judging rural Ireland by these dance blurbs, one would imagine that the entire population are returned emigrants who spent their lives in the neon-spangled honky-tonks of the tough San Francisco waterfront. However congested the district it is one long list of dances, monster dances, grand annual dances, stupendous carnival dances, gala dances, cinderellas, excuse-me's, even an odd 'Irish and Old Time' for the cranks. Only the odd name of man or place gives a pathetic clue that there is some make-believe in progress and that the newspaper is *not* one of the English language sheets of abandoned Shanghai. You are asked to dance out the Old and dance in the New 'to the haunting strains of Mulvaney's Rhythmic Swingsters'. What do you make of 'Farmers annual dance (cocktail bar)'? Personally, I see no reason why our ruined farmers should not wear tails if they want to, but they have been misled if they think it is necessary to forsake good whiskey or beer for lethal noggins of chemical gin. 'Lime, flood and spot lighting installed for the occasion by the Strand Electric Co., Dublin. Carnival Hats, Novelties and Gifts for Everyone. A Night of Laughter, Gaiety, Fun and Surprise.' *Where?* In TUBBERCURRY! This notice appears in the paper upside down and the reader is finally warned that the dance 'will be as crazy as this adver-

tisement'. At the Mayo Mental Hospital Staff Dance 'the floor
will be specially treated for the occasion,' while that other
dance in Fethard will be in aid of 'noteworthy object'.

Taking rural Ireland to include the towns, there are three or
four kinds of dances. For any dance costing over five shillings,
you must put on what is known as 'immaculate evening dress'.
You are on the border-line when you come down to 3/9. A
surprising number of young men own a passable dress-suit and
work-a-day rags, with absolutely nothing in between except
football attire. I have heard of dancing men being married in
their evening clothes.

The dress dance in the country is run by those of the white
collar and the white soft hand — clerks, merchants, doctors —
and is usually taken locally to be a proof of progress or culture.
When the plain people see handsome men in 'immaculate'
evening clothes alighting from fine motor-cars and disappearing into a Town Hall that seems temporarily glorious and re-
born, they know well from their cinema that there is city
devilry afoot. Inside, however, the scene is very familiar. Think
of an ordinary good dance (say in the European quarter of
Shanghai) and then divide everything by two. The lighting is
poor and the place is too hot. The floor is of thick planks (it
was put there to accommodate a welcome for Parnell) and the
knots will tell through the city man's shoddy pumps. The band
may be good or bad. Bands vary enormously for this reason —
*a dance is regarded as successful according to the distance the
band has to travel.* For the best possible dance the band would
have to come from India. This is the great immutable law that
determines the local prestige of every event. A Committee is
doing pretty well if they can get a band from a hundred miles
away. What is regarded as a good band in the country will have
'own electric amplification' but may lack a piano. Their tunes
will be old and grey and far behind the whistling repertoire of
any diligent cinemagoer. 'Good-night, Sweetheart' is still a rage
in the west.

Nearly every male who goes to dances likes drink and takes
plenty of it. Some people may think this is an offensive state-
ment but it is the plain truth. It is often a case of little by
little. There is no evil intention. It starts with a few half-ones
merely to get into form and after that the reveller is on his way,
even if he doesn't know where he is going. This part of the

evening's work is performed in an adjacent hotel or pub. Nearly every pub is entitled to serve a toothful to 'travellers' but in practice very few of the locals fail to obtain suitable filling for their teeth. It is an old custom.

This custom carries with it an odd accomplishment that no stranger can acquire. It is the craft of going out for twenty separate drinks to a pub 400 yards away without ever appearing to have left the hall at all. It is a waste of time seeking to solve this puzzle by observation. If you are a lady, you can dance every dance with the one gentleman, talk to him unremittingly in the intervals and yet you will notice him getting gayer and gayer from his intermittent but imperceptible absences. If, on the other hand, you are a man who is seated in the pub all night concerned only with honest drinking, you will observe the complementary miracle and wonder how the inebriate in tails manages to satisfy all the requirements of his partner in the hall without ever appearing to leave the pub. There it is. I can offer no explanation.

These dress dances are not very interesting. They have scarcely any relation to 'the dance hall scandal,' 'the jazz mania,' or any other popular explanation of the decay of our country at the present time. The real thing is the cheap dance where the price of admission ranges from 3d. to 1/6. To arrive at some idea of this, you must divide that recollection of Shanghai, not by two, but by high numbers that go higher as the price comes down. Most of the halls I have seen are old school-houses or new timber structures with a tin roof. There is no means of ventilation save the savage and heroic expedient of the open window. There is no attempt at having a proper dance floor, even where the hall has been built *ad hoc*. Light is provided by large paraffin lamps suspended from the roof, less frequently by incandescent paraffin installations on the walls. The music may be supplied by a solitary melodeon or piano-accordion, with possibly a fiddle and drums. Dance music as such is almost unknown. What seem to be vague recollections of Irish airs are churned out in an interminable repetition and nearly always bashed into a desultory three-four time that usually sounds very alien to what was intended by our ancestor. Even when a modern dance tune is attempted, it is played straight with no attempt at syncopation, and, being necessarily played from hazy memory, it sometimes finds itself mysteriously transformed into 'Terence's Farewell to Kathleen'.

The dancing itself is of the most perfunctory order. If the hall is small and the crowd enormous (and this is the normal situation) the parties quickly lock themselves into a solid mass and keep shuffling and sweating for ten minutes in the space of a square foot, like a vast human centipede marking time. If the hall is roomy and the crowd small, the dancers shuffle about in great circles and can travel a considerable distance in the course of an evening. If a lad cycles twenty miles to a dance and twenty miles home and does another ten miles in the hall, he is clearly in earnest about his dancing.

Just as the success of a dear dance depends on the extra-territoriality of the band, no cheap dance can be said to have succeeded if the door of the hall can be readily opened from without after the first half-hour. The crowd inside must be so dense that an entire re-packing and re-arrangement of the patrons is necessary before even the blade of a knife could be inserted through the door. When you do enter, you find your-self in air of the kind that blurts out on you from an oven when you open it. All about you is an impenetrable blue tobacco haze that is sometimes charged with a palpable fine filth beaten up out of the floor. Whether standing or dancing, the patrons are all *i bhfastodh* (Editor:- i.e., 'in a clinch') on each other like cows in a cattle truck, exuding sweat in rivers and enjoying themselves immensely. Nobody is self-conscious about sweat. It rises profusely in invisible vapour from all and sundry and there is no guarantee that each cloud will condense on its true owner.

There are certain general considerations which apply to all these dances. The girls always predominate and usually pay their own way. Behind the upright throng one can sometimes glimpse a low flat row of sitting people who look as if they were painted or pasted on the walls. Once there, they seem to have no chance of budging till the dance is over. There is always an official charged with accomplishing a hospitable rite known as 'looking after the band'. Late in the night there are signs on him that he has been looking after himself, but the boisterous revival of the 'musicianers' towards the end of the evening will prove that he has not made undue depredations on the trust fund. For a dance of any importance (say, a shilling dance) the average farmer's son will permit himself a half-pint of

'parliamentary whiskey' on the hip and will not hesitate to lace
his blood with judicious nips of poteen if the stuff is to be had.
The liquor is consumed in breath-taking gulps in a place apart
and is never openly flaunted. Scenes of open or riotous
drunkenness are rare. Notwithstanding any cloakroom that may
be provided, complete with attendant, the general tendency is
to bring the overcoat into the hall. No tax is payable on any
dance that costs anything up to 4d. Tax and licensing provisions
are evaded by calling a short dance a 'practice' or a 'dance
class'. Where supper is provided, the beverage is always tea,
never a nourishing or cooling draught like home-made
lemonade. If a committee can rise to the swirling device that
throws pretty and romantic coloured lights throughout the
darkened hall, they are entitled to call their functions 'gala
dances'. There are fine big halls here and there where dancing
is attempted on a reasonable basis − the big converted railway
shops at Dundalk, for instance, or the shirt factory building
outside Buncrana.

Irish dancing is a thing apart. There is perhaps one *céilidhe*
held for every twenty dances. The foxtrot and the Fairy Reel
are mutually repugnant and will not easily dwell under the
same roof. Very few adherents of the 'ballroom' canon will
have anything to do with a jig or a reel. Apart from the fact
that the Irish dance is ruled out in most halls by considerations of space or perspiration, there is a real psychological
obstacle. It is a very far cry from the multiple adhesions of
enchanted country stomachs in a twilight of coloured bulbs
to the impersonal free-for-all of a clattering reel. Irish dancing
is emotionally cold, unromantic and always well-lighted.

One occasionally encounters the barn-dance. This is the
'mind the dresser' business held to the tune of a lone Raftery
in a farmhouse kitchen, to celebrate a wedding or an American
wake. Most of the dances are sets and half-sets based on English
figure dances and introduced to this country in the seventeenth
and eighteenth centuries by the landlord class. There are also
boisterous versions of Irish dances and an odd invitation to
talented individuals to 'oblige' with solo items. Curiously
enough, this sort of thing is beginning to smell of the stage
Irishman.

Some district justices have a habit of taking leave of their
senses at the annual licensing sessions. They want Irish dancing

and plenty of it, even at the most monster 'gala dance'. They
believe that Satan with all his guile is baffled by a four-hand reel
and cannot make head or tail of the Rakes of Mallow. I do not
think that there is any real ground for regarding Irish dancing
as a sovereign spiritual and nationalistic prophylactic. If there is,
heaven help the defenceless nations of other lands.

Little need be said about dancing in Dublin or Cork. In Cork
nearly all the fun is concentrated in the spacious and well-run
Arcadia. Dublin has six or seven hotel-halls where the all-
important 'refreshment' facilities are available and some sixty
other halls where there is dancing several nights a week. In
addition, every junta of goodtime folk who care to register
themselves as a sports or social club can dance and drink almost
without restriction. In theory, only members can join in this
diversion but in practice anybody can pay and enter. At 1 p.m.
on Sunday morning these haunts are crowded with ill-slept
revellers in search of healing ale.

Yes, strange and beautiful sights you will see at a dance in
Dublin. Even a district justice, happy and mum, surrounding
with his righteous tissue a sizzling tank of malt. That dance,
however, does not cost threepence. The entry-fee is 7/6 or half
a legal guinea.

FLANN O'BRIEN was the name that many-sided literary genius put to
his novels and plays. His own name was Brian O'Nolan and he was born in
Strabane, Co. Tyrone in 1912. He was also known as Brother Barnabas,
George Knowall, the Great Count O'Blather etc. etc. but perhaps his best
known materialisation was as Myles na gCopaleen, the creator of the *Irish
Times* column *Cruiskeen Lawn* which first appeared about the same time
as *The Bell*, (October 1940) and ran up until his death in 1966. Flann
O'Brien was already known to the grateful few as the author of the cult-
novel, *At Swim-Two-Birds* (1939) and there was great excitement when in
the Sixties there appeared three more novels, *The Hard Life* (1961), *The
Dalkey Archive* (1964) and the rediscovered *The Third Policeman* (1967).
The pieces written for *The Bell* reflect his continuing interest in the sports
of the plain people of Ireland of the period: drink, dog-racing and dancing.

THE DANCE HALLS   *Flann O'Brien*   *February 1941*

SAINT PATRICK AND LAGER BEER

By LYNN DOYLE

THE district of Ulster in which I spent my childhood was about half Unionist and half Nationalist; that is to say half Protestant and half Catholic; for in those days, and I think even yet, our political opinions were decided by our religion. I *have* heard of Protestant Home Rulers, and — though not so often — of Catholic Unionists; but both were looked on with suspicion even in the camp which they had joined. It was the general feeling that there was something wrong with them, some hidden reason not quite creditable, as if a hen should go in swimming with the brood of young ducks she had hatched out.

But on one day of the year mutual ill-feeling was almost wholly laid aside — Saint Patrick's Day. This temporary unity was effected by the Saint chiefly through the rite known as Drowning the Shamrock. As the drowning was accomplished by means of whiskey it was carried out with enthusiasm by both creeds, sometimes in each other's company; Protestant antipathy to ritual being symbolized by absence of the shamrock. My kindly old Orange friend Ezekiel Henderson — bountiful bestower of pence, and even of three-penny-bits, on a sweet-greedy little boy — was a temperate man. Yet he drank whiskey three times a year; and once expounded to me the reason: "At Christmas, young fellow, for my religion; at the Twelfth of July to the glorious, pious, and immortal memory of you know who; and at Saint Patrick's Day in honour of ould Ireland."

But I must acknowledge that there was sometimes too much drinking on Saint Patrick's Day in our neighbourhood. Sometimes trouble came of it, comedy or tragedy; but mostly comedy.

The yardman on my uncle's farm, one Paddy Haggarty, was small of stature, and of a peaceful disposition when he was sober, which, indeed, he generally was. Under the influence of porter, his favourite drink, he remained modest and inoffensive, and developed an unexpected and pawky humour that amused even my aunt, who, for excellent reasons, was not sympathetic to drinkers. But when Paddy drank whiskey his character changed, and very much for the worse. He became red-faced and 'raised'-looking, a heated and provocative partisan of his Catholic faith, and extremely perverse and obstinate in all his opinions and doings. Our first ploughman of those days, a grave, still man, and slow to anger, was once moved to declare that when in his cups Paddy would have angered a duck.

About this time Paddy's courtship of our servant-maid Anne Blayney was going on. I paid a good deal of attention to the love-affairs of our maids when I was a child, and must without knowing it have gathered a considerable stock of information about love (though I cannot remember that it was of much use to me when I grew up), and received many confidences, probably because I was a patient and sympathetic listener, and always advised what the girl had already decided to do. It was therefore natural that Anne should consult me in a certain difficulty connected with her admirer, Paddy. Anne was a quiet, self-possessed little body — the first ploughman said she was the makings of so good a wife that no one would ever marry her — and Paddy's occasional whiskey drinking was a worry to her staid mind. It wasn't so much the smell of the stuff, she told me; though she didn't care for that, particularly at second-hand; but it made Paddy carnaptious, and that wasn't like him. Not that it was her business. Paddy was above her in many ways, she knew, with his book-reading and his learned talk. There was no doubt, saving my presence, he had put Dick Murray in his place about the five sacraments. He would never marry down to the likes of her, she felt in her heart; but, even if another woman should get him, she wouldn't ever like to hear of Paddy making a fool of himself. It would be altogether out of the question for her to say anything to Paddy; but would I say a wee word if I got the chance and try if I could get him to sign the pledge, even if it should be only against whiskey? She added that I would have a better chance of success if I waited until the day after he had been taking a sup.

I agreed that this would be the best time, and found my
opportunity the second day after Christmas, when Paddy was
a more than usually suitable subject for missionary zeal. Paddy
even anticipated my purpose. I needn't say a word, he told me.
He had learned his lesson this time, for good; and knew now
that porter was the only drink fit for a human being. This unexpected attitude of Paddy's disconcerted me not a little; but I
was an earnest child, and not to be satisfied with half-measures.
I painted a lively picture of the evil consequences of drinking
at all (of which, indeed, I had a good deal of knowledge, part of
it drawn, as I was careful to tell him, from Paddy himself), and
wound up with what I still think was the most adroit argument
that no sensible girl would ever have anything to do with a man
who wasn't a teetotaller.

I could see that Paddy was a good deal shaken by the
reference to Anne which he must have known I intended. He
sat for a long time without saying anything, and I thought
looked a little disconsolately at an empty porter-bottle on the
shelf of his sleeping room. Then he asked me to remember that
he didn't often take drink except at set-times, when a man
wants to be like everybody else; but gave in that I was a by-
ordinary wise child for my years, and that there was a lot in
what I had said. He would think it over, he told me.

He did think it over, and to some purpose; for, about a
fortnight after, Anne came to tell me that Paddy had gone
before Father B——— and taken the pledge. Her eyes were
shining, and she was deeply moved. I thought she was making
too great a fuss of what Paddy had done. But I had told her
about my sermon to him, laying stress on the last head of it;
and now, having in the meantime gained still more experience
in these matters, I see Anne was uplifted because Paddy thought
so much of her good opinion.

But there was one provision in the pledge which puzzled
Anne a good deal, and made her uneasy. Father B———, as
became his office, had been more merciful than I, and had
allowed Paddy liberty to drink lager beer. He was not
acquainted with the properties of this beverage himself; nor was
Paddy, at first hand; but a friend of large experience in liquors
had told Paddy that it was as good as teetotal, that a man could
consume a hogshead of it and still walk a single rail, and that,

so far as he was concerned he would near as soon drink water; and Father B——— hearkened to this expert. I put it to Anne that Father B——— must be supposed to know more than either of us (though privately I am afraid I smelt Catholic laxity) and Anne agreed. Nevertheless, she told me, she would be easier in her mind when the first set-day was over.

St. Patrick's Day was the next public holiday; and Paddy, according to his custom, put on his Sunday clothes and set out for the town of C———. He did not take formal farewell of Anne, but as he left the farm-yard he waved his hand toward the kitchen-door of the dwelling-house as if he expected Anne to be there, which indeed she was, with myself peering under her arm. She told me Paddy was coming home by the short-cut along the railway-line, and that she was to meet him at the level-crossing at seven o'clock. Then she asked me would I please walk in the direction of the crossing gates a little after seven. If I saw Paddy and her walking together, and she did not wave her handkerchief, I was to keep away, and let on I didn't see them; but if she waved her handkerchief I was to come over, and stick to them till they came back to the yard. I was a little surprised, because, not long before, Anne had told me with some hesitation that perhaps it would be just as well if I didn't always accompany her when she was going to meet Paddy. Then I became aware that Anne, like myself, thought Paddy (who had been altogether abstemious since Christmas) might try his new drink for the first time that day; and that, in spite of the sanction of the church, she still felt a little uneasy about how the experiment might turn out.

Though we said nothing to each other at the time, Anne and I found the day very long. At a quarter to seven Anne set out along the field-path to the crossing; and ten minutes later I followed. As I turned the last corner and came in sight of the crossing gates here was Anne running toward me along the field path at top speed, and sobbing as she ran.

'Oh, Master L———,' she cried, 'Paddy has got drunk on that queer stuff and is lying snoring on the lines, and won't budge; and the up train is due at a quarter past. Come quick; for he'll listen to *you*.'

But, when I went, Paddy would not listen to me, or to anyone else. I don't believe he would have listened to Father B———, or to any other dignitary of the Church except the

Supreme Pontiff, for whom as an Ulster Catholic he was at all
times, but notably in his cups, a potential martyr. Paddy was
lying on his back between the rails of the up line. His coat and
waistcoat lay beside his head, roughly folded; and he had taken
off his boots. He was very red in the face and snoring heavily.
Two empty black bottles lay near him. Their contents must
have consummated his ruin. And, as Anne had said, he wouldn't
budge. Certainly not for me, though I shook him with all my
childish might, and holloed in his ear. I don't think he knew
me; and I am certain he didn't know Anne, or he would have
yielded to her entreaties. But all he would do was to groan
and turn away when we pulled at him, and to snarl incoherently
but angrily, though still keeping his eyes shut.

At the end of ten minutes or so of continuous struggle we
were both very much exhausted. Over and over again we had
almost succeeded in dragging Paddy off the line; but at the last
minute he always managed to pull himself free and settle down
again to his uncomfortable slumber. By this time I had cried
myself almost sick, and was nearly as angry with Paddy as
scared about his possible fate. But Anne, though white in the
face and with desperate eyes, remained calm and patient. She
even found forethought enough to remove Paddy's coat and
waistcoat and boots to the margin of the line. Still, time was
passing swiftly. I could see her desperation growing; at which I
blubbered more hysterically than ever. The up train was now
actually due. But this was by my ten-shilling watch, which,
owing to my ministrations, wasn't to be depended on. Suddenly
Anne gave up her efforts and caught me by the arm. A strange
thought had come to her, a thought that in any other part of
the world would have been considered lunatic.

'Master L———' she said. 'There's only one thing rouses him,
when he's full. You know' — she hesitated — 'you know what
he split Dick Murray's ear for?'

I did know; and paused in my crying to nod my head.

'If I shouted in his ear and ran, he might follow me,' Anne
said. She bent over Paddy, then lifted her head without
speaking, and looked at me piteously — 'I can't say it, Master
L———' she said. 'Not if it was to save his life. There could be
no luck follow it. You do it,' she besought me, dragging at my
sleeve. 'It means nothing to you.— Quick Master L——— Shout
in his ear and run. — Oh quick; I hear the train.'

I still think the last sentence was Anne's cunning, bestowed on her by love. But I had no time for thinking then.

I put my lips to Paddy's ear. No moss-trooper ever holloed his slogan louder or more shrill than I delivered the blasphemous orison against the Supreme Pontiff. I trust my act will not be imputed to me for unrighteousness. In any event, my true intention was served. The half-conscious brain of Paddy Haggarty — so mighty is a ruling passion — dragged him swaying to his feet — 'To Hell with ould Billy,' he crowed back huskily, fumbled to take off, or button, his coat for battle, and pitched on his face clear of the lines.

The up line is straight for half-a-mile before it reaches the level crossing, and I know now that the engine driver would have seen us in good time. But neither Anne nor I had thought of that, and we hugged each other in a frenzy of relief and thankfulness, which presently somewhat abated in Anne when she saw the state of Paddy's Sunday trousers. We had dragged Paddy — for some reason much easier to handle now — over to the grassy margin of the railway. There he slept till almost nine o'clock, Anne and myself keeping guard. When he stirred and rose to his feet we watched him with beating hearts as he climbed heavily over the crossing gates; and then we made off home by the county road. My aunt scolded us for missing our supper. I don't remember what story we told her; but I know there was nothing in it about Paddy Haggarty or lager beer.

'LYNN DOYLE' was the pen-name of Leslie Alexander Montgomery who was born in Downpatrick in 1873. He became a bank-manager and used his experiences there (always a good source of 'crack') in the many humorous stories he wrote about County Down and especially about his home town known forever to literature as 'Ballygullion'. In all he wrote nine books about the place with such noted characters as Mr. Anthony the solicitor, Mr. Wildridge of the Bank and Patrick Murphy the narrator of the often uproarious tales. The first Ballygullion book was published in 1908, the last in 1957. Doyle interest is not confined to contemporary Ireland: like many Ulstermen he was fascinated by the United Irishmen of 1798 and wrote some excellent stories about them. He also tried his hand with less success at full-length novels. His pen-name came from his days with The Ulster Literary Theatre which Bulmer Hobson and David

Parkhill began in friendly rivalry to the Irish Literary Theatre ('Damn Yeats, we'll write our own plays'.) As Barry Fitzgerald was to find later, it was judicious in a 'respectable' community to use a cover for one's play-acting. Montgomery, as a bank official in Ulster, could not risk overt association with rogues and vagabonds so he signed his first full-length play, *Love and Land* (1914) with the code name 'Lynn C. Doyle' which in time was used without the 'C'. He was the first writer appointed to the Censorship Board but he resigned in 1937. He died in 1961.

SAINT PATRICK AND LAGER BEER   Lynn Doyle   *March 1941*

THE BREADMAKER

By BRYAN MacMAHON

NOREEN spilled the flour from the saucer to the losset, then slowly sieved it through her fingers. She clapped her hands dustily and walked to the yawning bin with its hoard of golden meal and silvery flour. She extracted a pinch of soda from a drab paper bag, then locked the pinch in the palm of her left hand. Back at the table again she crunched the soda over the flour. Now for the salt. Soda, salt, butter! All in? Then she walked to the dresser, took up a jug of sour milk and sniffed it. Her left hand was groping abstractedly for an empty jug while her eyes were examining the milk. She hummed as she sent the sour milk careering in a viscid bubbling waterfall from full jug to empty jug and back again. The ingredients of her cake had spoken in different voices: the flour had uttered the faintest flicker of a whisper, the soda had rustled as a nun's dress, the dampish salt had evoked water from the bases of her teeth, and now the thick milk gurgled with a lewd drunken joy. "Glug-glug-glug" it said, as the hiccoughing of a fat old toper. Laying down the jugs, Noreen gathered the feet of her irregular hillock of flour and made a rough crater at the top. Then she poured the milk into the mouth of the little volcano. Bubbles winked and broke, winked and broke, winked and broke. Short lives they had; one solitary violet-indigo-blue-green-yellow-orange-and-red wink and life was over. Birth, prime, old age. Pouff – so!

The old man and the old woman were seated by the fire under the dark cavernous chimney in the farm-house kitchen. The old man was opposite the girl who was making the cake, arrogantly watching her movements out of his red wicked eyes. He noted every feature of the pretty face that was framed in errant ringlets, and noting, he scowled. Scowled again as he looked at the interloper. Turning his face to the fire he railed inwardly at the thought of his big eedjit of a son. What right had Johnsey to go against his parents? What call had he to break the law that was there since time-out-of-mind that decreed that parents should match younglings in pub-snugs? What title had he to burst out laughing when a person mentioned the sanctity of a solicitor's settlement. A settlement was a grand thing entirely at the end of old folks' days. Sure it read as finely as a prayer and it gave spent people a last grandeur and importance: "Reserving unto the said John Joseph O'Sullivan, Senior, and to his wife Anne O'Sullivan during their lives the east room in said dwellinghouse with full right of ingress and egress through the kitchen of said dwellinghouse—"

Oho, the old man mused, but this purty-faced lassie had spoiled all that, a clever little schemin' slut if ever there was one, a regular doxy who had cajoled their fine broad Johnsey to the altar, a cute little cabaire with her white apron-strings making the cross of Calvary on her back. A white apron might be all right in the doctor's house in town where she was in service, but here in a farm house——! A bould little madam, faith she was, and the divil a stim of shame on her to walk into a snug warm place without a copper to cross herself with. And what harm but the money badly wantin' to fortune off Nellie in Dublin! Ah, but the good God was in His high sky, and she'd be tamed for it. Cut the ear down off him if she wasn't tamed for it before Christmas night was in the door——

His wife, who was rocking herself forwards and backwards on the sugan chair opposite him, looked apprehensively at her man. Seeing the bitterness in his face, her head revolved on unmoving shoulders, the better to view the breadmaker. Then with a trembling hand she groped among the voluminous folds of her skirts. A slash of red flannelette showed momentarily, and then the old hand emerged grasping a shiny penny mustard-box. With nose twitching peevishly in anticipation, the old wife extracted a pinch of snuff.

"Go ndeanfaidh Dia trocaire ar h-anaman na marbh," she intoned, as if it were a curse instead of a prayer.

"Amen," said the breadmaker blithely if not provocatively. The old woman resented the "amen". More so the old man, since it was his prerogative to answer her. A collie was lying with his nose in the cold ashes. It had one eye blue and the other brown. The old man struck it full across the forehead with his stick. "G'our that!" he said savagely. The dog fled howling, shaking his head humanly and sniffing strongly through his nostrils.

Open-mouthed the old woman swayed on her chair. Sneezed.

"Dia linn," she wheezed instinctively.

"Dia linn is Muire," chirped the breadmaker, even before the web of spittle from the crone's chin to her chest had broken.

Recovering from her sneeze the old woman scowled. The old man scowled in sympathy with her. The dog whimpered from the doorway.

"Poor Chep," Noreen said, "Poor oul' Chep."

For all the gay mask on her face the newly-married girl was deeply troubled. She knew well how completely the old pair were allied against her. Worse still, she fearfully recalled the flamin' lie she had told Johnsey, her own big soft Johnsey. That night under the ivy of the parsonage wall when, with her moonlit face upturned to his, he had entreated her not to laugh at his question. For himself he didn't care a ramblin' damn, but she knew that the ould wan'd keep pickin' at him till he'd get an answer. Could she bake a cake of bread? And Noreen recalled in horror how glibly the lie had come to her lips and how easily she had added to the lie. Who else baked all the bread in Dr. Mangan's? Was it for her good looks Dr. Mangan kept her? Would he like to ask Mrs. Mangan if he didn't believe her? And then, before her false dignity could run away with her, Johnsey's lips were sealed on hers and the incident was forgotten.

Retribution was come upon her now with a vengeance. Noreen became her own accuser. She who had never whitened her hands with flour in her life, who had done little else at the

Doctor's except to bob and bow to the red-faced and white-faced patients. To tell the truth of it, what was she but a la-di-da who had nothing to do but say "yes'm" and "no'm" and "ma'am, if you please," with an occasional mincing variation of "Who shall I say called?" And to make matters a hundred times worse, 'twas the first decade in that bogawn Johnsey's bead to boast of her breadmaking prowess to his mother. And, of course, the headstrong Johnsey refused the account of a match from the Fitzgerald girl of the New Glebe, who was a sow of a woman for all her father's long-tailed purse. Noreen faltered. Here she was, the liar, making a liar of Johnsey before his mother, who was the best breadmaker in the seven parishes. For men are born with "green hands," and they are gardeners; and people come into the world with rhythm at the tip of tongue and finger and they are musicians; and now and again, once in a generation perhaps, God vouchsafes to grant a woman power over fire and flour, and she is a breadmaker — the Breadmaker. Such a one was the old crone on the hearthstone — Johnsey's mother. Sure there wasn't a housewife in the barony who begrudged her her gift. Going by the road with their men in the orange-red market rails, the jealous women would open the wings of their shawls to blind their men to red-white discs of bread on O'Sullivan's sill. All kinds of bread came lickalike to Anne O'Sullivan — "stampy," griddle-bread, potato-cake, wholemeal-bread, currant-bread, caraway-seed bread, soda-bread, or the golden, crumbly, meal-bread called "Paca," after the good ship "Alpaca," which was the first ship to bring maize to Ireland in famine days. Aye, all breads came second nature to Annie Jack Sullivan — The Breadmaker.

As if divining the girl's thoughts, the old woman glanced again over her shoulder at the face of the breadmaker, then to the ungainly lump of dough on the losset. She turned again to the blaze and leaning forward she emitted the full of a tablespoon of spittle. It flattened to a starry design on the broad flag of the hearth. Venemously she drew her boot across it as if to show the contempt a true breadmaker had for the white poison of the shops. And already her mind was framing bitter equivocal phrases with which to wound the new breadmaker. Long-loved jibes rolled in her mouth and jostled one another to secure first place in the queue of maledictions on her tongue's tip.

The oven was squatting on the embers. Into it Noreen threw the ungainly mass of dough, made the sign of the Cross on it with a knife, in the name of the Father, Son and Holy Ghost, stabbed once in each of its four quadrants. Then she lifted the lid with the tongs and put the cover on the pot-oven. Next she squashed red coals on the lid. With heat-reddened face she straightened herself. 'Twas done! Flesh and blood could do no more. Now her cause was beyond human strivings. Her fate was in the lap of God: her firstling was leaping in the womb of the fire.

Now to wait. The old breadmaker, the young breadmaker, the old breadmaker's bitter man.

Now to wait.

Hens' meat to be got. Noreen got it. Bonavs and sucky-calves clamouring for their food. Noreen fed them. The black braddy cow to be milked before the red udder-troubled herd lumbered down from the bawn field. Noreen milked her. Then she went into the kitchen to raise the cover of the oven to see how her cake was doing.

The old woman leaned forward farther and farther as Noreen took the tongs in her hand. The old man's jaws fell apart and a thin quick dribble ran down on his greasy lapels Noreen muttered to herself as if she had forgotten something, smiled impishly and laid aside the tongs. Then she almost ran out to the piggery, to vent her pent-up laughter. The old woman clucked angrily in her disappointment. The old man grasped his stick firmly and the watchful dog, who had resumed his place in the ashes, fled yelping before the blow could fall.

Again the fireside pair settled themselves to wait. Their eyes were glued on the oven. After a space Noreen came in again and busied herself mightily with the stitched delph on the dresser. Laying aside a large ancient dish she took up an alarm-clock which would go only when lying on its face, studied it minutely, then raised her gaze to the black roof-joists as if she were solving an abstruse problem. The old woman looked at her with a false smile that did its best to be triumphant. The old man was torpidly scraping dirt from between two floor-flags with the feruled end of his hazel staff. Noreen smiled benignly at the poll of the old man and rather archly at the face of the old bean-a'-tighe, though within her tremulous breast she could hear a voice piping shrilly through the halls of Heaven for the

succour of a saint who knew something of the craft of breadmaking.

At long last she tightened the soldier-sashes of her apron,
which were so becoming in the house in town but which seemed
so completely out of place in the rude farm kitchen. She sighed
at the change in her way of living, but smiled as she thought
of her fine man above in the ploughland with the animate
draughtboard of gulls and crows about his shoulders, and the
red loam falling freely like meal from his silver coulter. She
grew warm and moist at the feeling of security, the feeling of
strength, the feeling of safety the touch of his body imbued.
But for him she could scarcely have the valour to wage this
smiling silent battle against the peevish pair by the fire. Not a
battle, she hastily amended, but a long weary war with no ally
by her, to be ended only when the old couple were side by side
in their coffins in the Kill of the Bees.

Ceasing some wholly petty business about the kitchen,
Noreen pursed her lips and emitted a faint sound of annoy-
ance. "Tck, tck," she went, as if upbraiding herself for her
forgetfulness. The old man's patience seemed to have become
frayed in the passage at arms. Noreen was now between the old
couple with the tongs in her hand. For a moment she toyed
with the notion of laying it down again, but seeing that the
collie was now hemmed in on the hearth and seemed
instinctively to accept her propinquity as proof of sanctuary,
she routed the idea from her mind. With great deliberation she
inserted the tip of the tongs in the loop of the lid and lifted it.
The two were craned forward in their sugan chairs, the old man
tapping eagerly on the hearthstone with his stick, the old
woman swilling saliva through her toothless gums. Up, up came
the cover, slowly, with the greyed coals quivering on its top.
Up. Then the old crone gasped, venomously released her spit
and sank back. The old man threw himself back heavily. It
was then Noreen lit with laughter. The cake, God bless it, was
so big, so lovely, so golden-brown. Oooh! A cloth. Tilt. Tilt
carefully. She knuckled it on its back and laughed at the little
resonance. Tested it with a knife-blade and almost crowed when
the blade came clean.

The Virgin never swathed Jesukin as carefully as Noreen
swathed her cake. First, with pride and reverence she lifted it
high above her head, as one would a child the better to gloat

on its beauty and fine limbs. Then, when it was well wrapped in a cloth, she placed the cake standing on edge of top of the bin.

In an access of impishness she broke out into a song the townies sang. She had only half of it, but the words "blue ukelele" were recurrent in the refrain. Well she knew that the words sounded abominably in her country mouth, but nevertheless she sang it as a crude hateful paean of victory over the old pair.

After Noreen had gone out into the farmyard the old man leered across at the deposed breadmaker. Old Annie Jack masked up her face in a narrow vindictiveness and sniffled like a wet hound. She pulled a crude kype up over her hair in token of defeat and fumbled in her skirt. The corners of her nose went crinkling again. Suddenly the old man's leering expression changed to one of peculiar loyalty. He looked back at the shrouded bread behind him. Then he looked craftily at his wife, who seemed sunken in the deepest senile despondency. He tapped on the flagstone to draw her attention; then, with his brightened eyes on the doorway, he leaned back and with a sudden push of his stick sent the cake skittling to the floor. It fell helplessly on its side and its swaddling clothes parted to show a broken cake spilling its steam on the air. The old woman cackled dryly and searched feverishly in her clothes for her snuff-box.

But the old man had not reached the end of his bravery. He raised his cracked voice.

"Hey, girlie!" he called.

The dog left the ashes and with a sudden snap took a hunk of the hot bread. Carried it under the table. Laid it on the floor. Licked it gingerly. Looked around with greedy canine sagacity. Growled.

"Well, sir?" The breadmaker was framed in the doorway.

Solemnly the old woman lifted a pinch of snuff to her nostrils. "Go-ndeanfaidh..." she began. Then the laughter broke on her.

BRYAN MacMAHON, born in Listowel in 1909 describes himself with bare adequacy as 'schoolmaster, novelist, university lecturer and balladmaker'. He first came into prominence in the pages of *The Bell* to which he contributed a dozen stories and among other essays a note on how he makes a ballad. All his work has tremendous vitality and a glory of rich words that lead to the pleasantest kind of intoxication. His best novels are *Children of the Rainbow* (1952) and *The Honey Spike* (1967) which previously had been a very successful play. Other plays that have been successful are *The Bugle in the Blood* (1949) and the odd fantastical *Song of the Anvil* (1960). But it is as a short story writer that MacMahon will best be remembered. There have been many of these and they have appeared in many periodicals and anthologies. *The Lion Tamer* (1949) contains the best of his early stories and there is a further excellent selection in *The Red Petticoat* (1955). Bryan MacMahon still lives in Listowel and as his most recent collection, *The End of the World* (1976) shows, the zest, the skill, the excitement have not gone from his writing. 'The Breadmaker' in its loving detail of ordinary life, its humour and above all in the superb flow of its telling is a very characteristic MacMahon story.

THE BREADMAKER   *Bryan MacMahon*   *August 1941*

CURTAIN UP
By LENNOX ROBINSON

WITH Lady Gregory's death the Theatre changes some-what. New Directors come and go, the Theatre's headed notepaper has constantly to be altered. It was time for a blood-transfusion. I know I thought that the way things had been done for fifteen or twenty years must be the right, the only way to do such things. Our procedure had over it the benediction of time. In cleaning up, as in all spring-cleanings, things were lost as well as gained.

People said, 'It is not the same Abbey'. I reply, 'It never has been'. I have heard that remark ever since nineteen hundred and ten. The audience, I am told, has grown stupid and laughs in the wrong place; it laughed equally wrongly in nineteen hundred and twelve. During the Anglo-Irish war patriotism ran so high that any patriotic sentiment expressed on the stage was received with prolonged applause, thus holding up the action of the play. I had to put a note on the programme warning the audience that the players had instructions to continue the play regardless of the applause. The applause stopped. In nineteen hundred and fifty people will lament the palmy days of nineteen thirty-five. Lately there have been grumblings at the second-rate quality of our new plays; turning back the pages of this book I see that I made exactly the same complaints to Yeats in 1918; his reply to me seems still apropos.

For me, only superficialities in the Abbey have altered. As long as I continue to meet Seaghan Barlow's stern face in the scene-dock, go to the green-room and find there Maureen Delaney, Eileen Crowe, F. J. McCormick, U. Wright and other dear faces the Abbey is much the same as ever it was. I am getting used to missing Jack Larchet from his seat at the piano. He came to that seat as a young man just about the time I joined the Theatre and was there for more than thirty years, and made our little orchestra the most distinguished for its size in Dublin. He quickly became too important a musician to spend every evening playing our curtain up and down, but he found it almost impossible to tear himself free, and when the parting finally came it would be hard to say whether the Abbey or John Larchet felt the wrench more keenly.

One thing seems not to alter — the quality of the acting. When I think of 'Abbey acting' my thought needn't go back to the nineteen-twenties, nor to the Arthur Sinclairs and Sara Allgoods of 1910, it can dwell on the acting I saw in the Theatre last week. For if it is true that we haven't found another Murray nor an O'Casey, we continue to find players just as good as those players of thirty years ago. After all these years of watching acting, of trying to teach it, of attempting to act myself, the thing remains a mystery. Inexplicable. Unplumbable. No one can be taught to act though a person may be helped to act. Voices can be developed, the range of notes in

the voice can be enlarged, movement can be taught, certain
technicalities can be learned, but the innermost thing, the spark,
the spring — call it what you will — remains a mystery. Stature
has nothing to do with it; Edmund Kean, according to Mrs.
Siddons, was 'a horrid little man... there was too little of him
to make a great actor' — this before he proved that he *was* a
great actor. Beauty has nothing to do with it. Rachel was an
ugly little woman with a harsh, hard voice. The player himself
is the last person who can explain the mystery, the last to be
able to offer an answer to the old, old question, 'Do you
genuinely "feel" your part, do tears fill your eyes even against
your will, to your consternation does your voice break, does
laughter bubble out of you spontaneously or is it all
deliberately planned a few seconds before the moment of your
tears, your laughter, your whatever-it-may be?' I believe that
the finest acting is unconscious, it springs from instinct. Is it
not analogous to the behaviour of the barnyard fowl? Hens have
so many different notes in their voice; the one which announces
the laying of an egg, the broody cluck, the very distinct cry
which calls the chickens to their food, the equally distinct cry
that warns of danger. Do not chickens hatched in an incubator,
chickens who have never seen a chick bigger than themselves —
not to speak of a hen — utter these exact cries when the proper
moment arises? Perhaps the whole scale of the emotions lies
latent within each one of us, and some of us have more easily
the power to evoke such and such an emotion, and then voice
and gesture and movement fit each other as the fingers to an
old glove. I once played Pirandello's mad king in *Henry IV*.
I had never seen a madman, nor did I visit an asylum for the
purpose of studying the symptoms of madness, yet certain
doctors who witnessed my performance said to each other,
'Look, he uses his hands just the way a madman does, no sane
person does those things with his hands'. I mention this not to
take credit for my acting, because unfortunately I don't know
for the life of me what I did with my hands. But indeed my
friends have been careful to give me little or no credit for any
acting I have done, acting which did not altogether depend on
my unconscious imagination, but which really involved much
thought and pains and hard work. But if I played a Strindberg
madman — *The Father* — they simply said, 'Well, of course
Lennox Robinson *is* mad, there's no acting in *that*.' And if I

sweated very hard over 'Lewis Dodd' — seven changes of raiment — 'But he's exactly that type, artistic and all that sort of thing. He's very good of course, but there's no acting there. He *is* Lewis Dodd.' But when I acted a God no one said that in real life I was divine...

When I came back to the Abbey Theatre as Manager I came back to a theatre very different from the one I had left. I had left it prosperous, with a fine company, lacking exciting plays, perhaps, but — given time — such plays would be sure to come. Instead came the war, that war which killed every repertory theatre in England and almost killed the Abbey. The audiences dropped... dropped. The players' salaries had to be reduced and further reduced; the stariest of the players sought their living elsewhere. Sara Allgood went, Arthur Sinclair went, and J. M. Kerrigan and Sidney Morgan. Finally, Fred O'Donovan left, taking with him the best of the players who were still left, and when I was asked to come back, just after the Armistice, there was but a handful of young players and a balance in the bank of one hundred pounds.

My only quarrel with A. E. Malone's excellent book, *The Irish Theatre,* is that he slurs over the Abbey's period from 1919 to 1925. To my mind those years (not, really, because I was so closely associated with them) were as gallant as any in the Theatre's history. As gallant as the earliest years of struggle. The war was over for England, but not for us. We had our Anglo-Irish war to face, later we had our Civil War. In the Anglo-Irish war we soon had a curfew, which moved slowly back from midnight to eight-thirty; finally our performances had to begin at five-thirty, but workers in the city preferred to hurry home at five and be safe from bombs and ambushes in their own gardens. (Of course the curfew had its compensations, the last June of the Anglo-Irish war was a very dry one and the water shortage was acute, no one was allowed to use a garden-hose, but the water-bailiff couldn't be on the road after nine o'clock, so the hoses played merrily until midnight).

For the sake of the players, in many cases entirely dependent on us for their livelihood, we had to try to keep the Theatre open. F. J. McCormick sold by degrees his dearly-prized library, Maureen Delaney implored me with tears to keep the Theatre going, she was ready to play the part in her repertory she most disliked (a part in one of my plays, by the way), she would play anything. We lost Arthur Shields, who went to London and the States and Australia to play *The White-headed Boy* — we didn't recapture his fine talent for some years — but still we hung on. Curiously, we never were raided by the British, not that there was anything for them to find, save props grown shabbier and shabbier and a wardrobe falling to pieces — a joy to the moths. We had to consider very seriously whether we could afford a 2/11½ blouse or a new cotton apron, Seaghan Barlow had to work miracles with warped flats. I forgot, the British might have found something, for about ten years ago a man came to me looking for a hand-printing press, it had been hidden in the Abbey, he said; it was the press on which the declaration proclaiming an Irish Republic had been printed. I was not at the Theatre in 1916, and neither I nor anyone else could trace the press.

We did not trim our sails in deference to Dublin Castle or the lorries of Black-and-Tans. Shortly after Terence MacSwiney s death, by hunger-strike, we produced his play *The Revolutionist*. It had been published some years before, it is not a very good play, but it has integrity and sets out all the ideals he died for. It is a bothering play to produce, having many changes of scene, and its dress-rehearsal was, more than usual, an occasion of work and worry. We were giving the play all the publicity we could, and there was a knot of camera-men present, and the American Consul and his wife had asked to be allowed to attend the dress-rehearsal rather than a public performance. After the second act I dashed behind to help to set the next scene, only to be confronted at the entrance to the stage by a very young man — almost a boy — dangerously dangling a revolver. He informed me that I couldn't go on the stage, to which I replied, 'What nonsense, I'm Manager here, and I'm producing this play,' and I brushed him aside. The players were in their dressing-rooms changing, they knew nothing about what was occurring, and I thought no more about it, but ten minutes later a miserable, shivering little English camera-man, his back against the wall in a corner of the stage, was surrendering his camera. He represented some picture-paper which had written sneeringly about MacSwiney and his hunger-strike, and it had been decided that the news-paper should not be allowed to produce photographs of the play. I believe his camera was returned a week or two later.

The American officials left very hurriedly, but they did not forget their manners, and the Consul's wife thanked me, in some agitation, for a delightful evening.

Apart from the fact that our tiny audiences were spelling financial ruin we had by 1921 again built up a fine company and some splendid new plays. Just after I came back, early in 1919, Barry Fitzgerald got his first good part. He had been one of those players who develop slowly. Sometimes a young aspirant will come to an audition or will play a small part, and at once you recognise immense possibilities. I am told that Fred O'Donovan was in that category, he leaped at once into parts of importance. So, certainly, was P. J. Carolan. I saw him first as a priest in the first rehearsal of *The Revolutionist,* the way he stood, the way he moved, the way he spoke marked him down as an actor of immense importance. Five minutes audition from Eileen Crowe was sufficient. But Maureen Delaney and Barry Fitzgerald had to feel their way, learning slowly and making many mistakes, but at last evolving the beautiful artists they are. It was in Lady Gregory's *Dragon* that Barry at last came into full flower, a rich, glorious performance; I forget Delaney's first blossoming. F. J. McCormick had got a few years earlier his first big chance as 'Larry Doyle' in *John Bull's Other Island,* and from that time on was to prove himself almost impeccable in small parts and big ones. A few years ago a thoughtful American woman spent her summer touring the theatres of Europe. She ended up with a few weeks in Dublin, and finally said to me: 'I have seen one or two finer performances than Mr. McCormick's but I have never seen such a versatile actor.' He can be Oedipus one week, Joxer Daly the next, Parnell, a drunken Professor Tim, a country jockey in *The Glorious Uncertainty* – years before, in America, some newspaperman asked me how many parts our principal players knew, and I enquired of Sara Allgood and Arthur Sinclair and the others. It transpired that they could go on the stage without a rehearsal in between forty or fifty parts, big and small. McCormick's repertory must be as big if not bigger...

Of the producers whose work I have had a chance of studying Granville-Barker's was the most completely efficient. But Yeats was more exciting. He did not know his stage as thoroughly as Granville-Barker, he had not the latter's advantage of having been an actor himself, he saw his plays as a series of pictures — and I have to admit that I have only seen him at rehearsals of his own plays, perhaps he was not so inspiring in other authors' work — but he had an unerring eye for movement and pose. Sometimes he asked for impossibilities from his players — but they were only impossible because the players' genius was not the full match for his. A rehearsal with him was a terror and an inspiration. Perhaps some day I shall write more fully of him as a man of the theatre, but not here. His death has evoked a wealth of reminiscence, I shall not add to it now. I have written of him on a few occasions since his death, and I tried to write an unofficial biography of him and failed. I was pen-tied. I think he was too supremely important to me for it to be possible to stand back and be dispassionate. From the day I met him to the day of his death he was the dominant personality in my life. There were times when I would see him every day, there were times when I wouldn't see him for months — it didn't much matter which. He was always there. His hand-writing on an envelope on my breakfast-table would make me tremble with fear and pleasure. Ten to one it would be about some trivial theatre matter, for he never wrote profundities to me. I am sure he despised my mind, though I know he liked some of my work, and pleased with *Crabbed Youth and Age*, dedicated a small book to me...

LENNOX ROBINSON was born in Douglas, Cork in 1886 and educated at Bandon Grammar School. His early absorption in music changed to drama fever after seeing the Abbey company on the visit to Cork in 1907. This same visit caused in him an ardent nationalism from which he never recovered, though he remained, as he wrote in a symposium for *The Bell* of June 1944 on 'Protestantism since the Treaty', 'a hopeless case from the Catholic point of view'. His work as manager and moulder of the Abbey and the excellence of his own plays have tended to be eclipsed by his close proximity to the giants of the Irish Literary Revival'. It was his decision to let the theatre stay open on the death of Edward VII (May 7, 1910) that caused Miss Horniman, the patron of the theatre, finally to lose her patience and return to England. Robinson wrote one novel, 'A Young Man from the South' (1917) but he is best known as the author of continuingly popular comedies such as *The Whiteheaded Boy* (1916) and *Drama at Inish* (1933). The success of these has diverted attention from his own excellent serious plays. During his professional life he was

noted for his kindness and encouragement to young writers. He died in
Dublin in 1958. The excerpt from his autobiography also called *Curtain
Up* (1941) shows the man at his most typical, elegant, self-effacing and
genuine in his love of country and art.

CURTAIN UP   *Lennox Robinson*   *September 1941*

A JUNE SUNDAY IN ARMAGH
By LESLIE GILLESPIE

O N Sundays we always rode girls' bikes, my Uncle and I.
Maybe that was because we were always so poor in the
country and bikes render better service in such circumstances by being hermaphroditic. The twin spires of the Roman
Catholic Cathedral towered over us the whole way into the
town. The bell in the Presbyterian Church on the Mall was
always striking for the last time when we stowed our steeds
away in the yard of the Beresford Hotel, which really was a
hotel and not merely a glorified publichouse as is so often the
case in country towns. A noisy clattering run through an entry
of wee white-washed houses brought us out on to the Mall, and
we more often than not took our places in the middle of the
first hymn, whereupon, before we had time to get a breath, a
considerate gentleman would sidle up and murmur 'seventy-
five' to us, or 'two-hundred-and-one,' or some such odd
number. Once I broke a convention by shuffling over and asking
a young girl: 'Miss, what's the number of the hymn please?'

I never listened to what the minister was saying. Occasionally
I made manful efforts, but always the effort of gazing fixedly
at a specific point for a long time eventually hypnotized me, till
I heard nothing but a droning, and saw nothing but a circle of
dancing lights. Everyone seemed to be in Heaven for a day.
Hats were so picturesque, the sun was so bright, faces so
radiant, the choir near-angels. There was the audible

background of the week-day — shouts from young ruffians racing greyhounds in the sunny cricket-fields across the Mall, and on the streets the dull thudding of hoofs and the jingling harness of morning milk-carts.

There were some men sitting in the pews around who were to Armagh as night is to day. Their faces had a leathery texture, and their stiff white collars declined to sit easily on their necks. In Sabbath costume they seemed to have a hangdog air and tomorrow at this same hour I used to visualise one of them on a hayrake and another squatting in a potato-drill.

Sunday afternoons were mostly dull — the sun was not shining. If it were shining I usually managed to slip out, call over for Billie, and together we went up to the Pert School-house where there was (and still is) a fine orchard chock-full of Beauties of Bath; or over to 'Camell's' (Campbell's) Hole in the Callan to have a 'plought'. Being a city man I never knew what this singular word meant, and was too ashamed to admit it; just as when I didn't know why people you met on the roads said — 'Good morra, bhoy!' when it was surely 'Good day!' If it were dull I was made to learn the verses of a hymn, and then snug on the sofa in the kitchen with Nero, the fox-terrier, curled up beside me and a rug thrown over us I solemnly set out to read 'The Vicar of Wakefield' or 'Gulliver's Travels'; or any book equally tested by the passing of innumerable Sundays and generations of self-esteemed church-goers, all happily afflicted like myself with the sweet malady known as 'spiritual neurasthenia'.

My dream was to get the hold of a school-story and eat it from cover to cover. One of these was Thomas Day's memorable 'Sandford and Merton', and it was only a few years ago that I discovered this to be a rare book of the last decade of the eighteenth century and by a novelist in direct lineage from Fielding to Scott. My Uncle and Aunt were likewise tucked up — in armchairs with footstools, and rugs wrapped round them and gold-rimmed spectacles on their noses. That looked so very queer because throughout the week they had no need for them, looking after hens, driving mowing-machines, directing the building of haycocks. My Aunt's favourite journal in 1927 was 'The Christian Herald', which is still going strong, and every Sunday my uncle perused 'Paradise Lost'. He assured me that he could repeat it from cover to cover without a

mistake. I got him started one day in the middle of a hay-
field, and sure enough he repeated the first book without
stopping, but in the second he stopped so many times that I
peremptorily advised him to give it up. My uncle was an
advanced man for his country, social position, age, decade. One
day he showed me a poem he had written. 'But there are no
rhymes in it,' I said. He smiled mysteriously and went on
pulling at the cow's teats.

There was hanging on the wall a picture of a vicious Victorian
fun-garden — Hampstead Heath on Bank Holiday — with
drunken men in it and loose women fraternising with them on
hobby-horses, and the streets were called 'Temptation Avenue'
and 'Vice Lane'. But I used to think that women in bustles
and muffs were so very respectable-looking (the contemporary
daring practice for females in 1927 being to wear skirts at the
knees) that it was ridiculous to attribute sin to them, and anyhow these painted, alien men and women in a London fun-
garden had nothing to do with the timeless countryside around
Armagh. I believe now that they were intended for young
servants alone in big cities in the time of Parnell. There was also
a photograph of Nurse Cavell with two big dogs, and that kept
telling us that the War still loomed very large. 'The War' held
me spellbound, and I pestered veterans to talk about it. They
never did. There was also 'the Troubles'. But I'll say nothing
about them.

I usually fell asleep, and sometimes I would wake up, and
looking from the window through the tangle of wild
blackcurrant that climbed all along the walls I could see the end
of the cow-shed with the big ash-tree beside it and a crow fixed
on the top like a sentinel, a swallow or two gliding about in the
moody sky, and I couldn't help feeling the strange brooding
stillness. The atmosphere was almost vacant, because the crowds
were absent, and there were no houses piled on each other.
There was a Bavarian clock on the mantel-piece, with a faded
sprig of holly in it from one end of the year to the other. I
could understand why my poor sister wanted to go to Church
again in the evening. She wanted to see and be seen by, what
was for her, the outside world. Poor Venie! She's far away in
Canada now.

I dozed off, and about five o'clock was awakened by Bridie
calling us into tea. There was always currant-cake, fruit-loaf,

and oranges and other delicacies. Before I got up I used to look
past the cow-shed, past McGurgan's on the hill, to Harrison's big
hay-shed in a clump of firs far away that always seemed to be
framed in that window at any hour or second of the daylight.
Beyond that again was Newry away behind the hills, and my
uncle used to point out a tiny line of thorns and trees with a
load of hay passing along it, and tell me that that was the
Dublin Road. Dublin was a hundred miles away, and it was
only a very second-class road to Dundalk. My uncle was
romantic-minded. Incidentally they only called it 'Harrison's',
for it belonged to Edmund James Litton. Mrs. Harrison was in a
private asylum; Samuel, the father, was dead, and Leo, one of
the boys, a good-looking fellow, but too fond of drink and the
women, had come home from Canada and ruined the place,
while his brother stayed on in Toronto. Barney, an affectionate
young calf, used to look over the hedge at me as I got up. He
was almost able to put his head inside the kitchen.

   The hour or so after tea till half-past six was nerve-racking
for me. I always tried to wriggle away before that hour.
Neighbouring men used to drop in casually and everything on
the face of the earth was discussed — especially religion,
politics, murder-trials, bacon-prices, and even hen-robberies.
Such things interested me too, but on a good evening the river,
Billie and the Blind Man's interested me more. At seven I was
considered a good reader and a prodigious scholar, 'who drank
the larnin',' and those old fellows kept me reading column after
column about K.C's and Juries in murder-trials and about
internal conditions in 'Roosia' (which was a word for them
and me equivalent to 'Hell') — till I was worn out. My aunt
placed spittoons at strategic intervals around the floor, and in
spite of her evident provision for his comfort George Allen
persisted in spitting on the mat. About nine Bridie brought in
the stout, just when the talk was focussing upon revolutions.
In their revolutions they never succeeded in getting beyond the
seventeenth century and the Glorious One of 1688. Once I
tried to introduce a vein of interest in the French one of 1789
and the Russian one of 1917, and was summarily told not to
blaspheme. George Allen was a pioneer of wireless in those
days, and he 'stoutly' maintained that 'it was the electricity in
the air that done it'. My uncle led them all an intellectual dance.
He amused himself by playing the role of a 'Jack! Jack! Show

your light!' but avoided all major dialectical tours de force.

I myself got away, called for Billie, and together we made our way up the road over Sheridan's Brae, past Dog Row to 'the Blind Man's'. His name was Ned Carr, and as he handed the Woodbine over the counter he used to say: 'Ah hope an' trust yous young fellows isn't goin' ti smoke them'. 'Naw Ned'. 'It's a bad habit,' as he scooped up the ha'pennies. There was a photograph of the Pope on the wall that we gazed on with a kind of frightened awe. Then up the Keady Road to Lizzie Bell's, where we had taken about ten acres of hay, and I used to go up like the 'grand wee man' everybody said I was and examine the snug haycocks to make sure that the big wind hadn't upset them and they weren't rotting with the rain. Sometimes she took us into the parlour and gave us apples, a room that was for looking at and only sitting in on very special occasions.

Down by Camell's home, with rats in the river, and the evening-colours of violets, crimson and russet-green. I used to shout at our Polly away up on Camell's stank, and she would raise her white head for a moment and then continue her grazing with the equine smile that I will swear is often in a horse's eyes. Down home along the railway-line and over the viaduct when, if we were lucky, we heard Tommie Hunter over at the beetling-mills playing 'The Road to the Isles' on the bagpipes. That music haunts me — along with summer-flies and the pine-trees and the glassy evening-expression of the river.

I usually entered the house when the politicians were at the door preparing to depart. They all gave me a dirty look and asked me one after the other why I ran away and didn't stay to 'edicate' my mind. My aunt, along with her dirtier look, gave me a bowl of porridge, and I hurried up the stairs into my sister's room, where was a small bottle of Californian Poppy that I loved to smell — lingeringly: it reminded me of my Uncle William, who had a fruit farm in Saint Catherines, near Toronto; and with the perfume and the thought of the distant fruit-farm mingling in my head I undressed, climbed into bed... and stayed awake, day-dreaming for hours.

LESLIE GILLESPIE was born in Belfast in 1920 but at the age of seven 'was rescued for a year from city streets and discovered the wonders of rural life in Armagh'. The piece printed here gives some idea of how golden that age was. Returned to Belfast he learned how to deal with the city. He went to Sullivan School, Holywood then a separate township on the south shore of Belfast Lough and thence to Queen's University where he was an active member of a group of young Ulster writers. His novel, *The Man from Madura* (1952) was based upon his experiences in India. He has written other novels, including *Decline in the West* and much theatrical journalism. At present he lectures in London University. He is engaged upon several biographies and a kind of Belfast 'Strumpet City'. His daughter is Elgy Gillespie, the *Irish Times* journalist.

A JUNE SUNDAY IN ARMAGH   Leslie Gillespie   *October 1941*

GALWAY
By DONAGH MacDONAGH

GALWAY
by Donagh MacDonagh

Galway called out of sleep,
And wakened the port of the mind,
And the islands that crouch on the water,
Hiding under the wind.

Sailed up properly.
Boats and gulls and turf-smoke
And a cliff high as Nelson
Called till I woke.

And cast all the symbols away
And thought of the Corrib in flood,
Rain hammering on the brain,
A town moored in mud.

DONAGH MacDONAGH was born in Dublin in 1912, the son of Thomas MacDonagh, the wittiest and most academic of the 1916 leaders.

He was equally well-known as a District Justice and as a literary fellow. His legal expertise stood him in good stead for his comic verse-play *Step-in-the-Hollow* (1957) which he adapted from *Der Zerbrochene Krug* (1806) by the German dramatist, Kleist. His play *Happy as Larry* (1947) made his name but some of his finest writing is to be found in his poetry. He edited (with Lennox Robinson) *The Oxford Book of Irish Verse* in 1958. He died in 1969.

GALWAY   *Donagh MacDonagh*   *October 1941*

SUMMER LOANEN
By SAM HANNA BELL

THE boy in the corduroy kneebreeches moved slowly down the sunny gnat-hung loanen, searching the sheughs for sourleek or wild strawberries. He turned each leaf carefully before he put it in his mouth, since the afternoon on Quinn's knowe when he had felt a little slippery body under his tongue.

The feathered quicken-grass and nodding goose-grass with its wheatlike head grew far into the loanen, making shaded arbours between the ancient blackthorn roots. It was the vivid crimson jersey of the boy which caught the strawberry hunter's eye. He sat with his back to the ditch, cushioned on the lush grass, and he juggled three white stones, letting them run through his fingers and fall on the ground between the crook of his chubby knees.

Although he could not have failed to hear the approach of the other, the boy on the bank did not raise his head. He seemed engrossed in lifting and tossing his polished pebbles, and all that the newcomer could see of his features were a tangled sphere of light sunbleached hair, the perspective of round ruddy cheeks, a snub nose appearing and disappearing behind his forehead fringe as he raised and lowered his head

with the juggling stones, and a glimpse of a sturdy sun-reddened
neck.

Around the ankle of the boy in the red jersey was fastened
a goat-collar and from it ran a long tether into the heart of a
boretree bush. The boy approached the seated figure, and
squatting down, cried in a friendly but excited voice, 'Hi, wee
lad, ye're tethered tae the dyke!' The long grass stirred a little
distance away and a little girl stumbled out of the hedge backward, her soiled chubby hands full of the stemless heads of
daisies, wild violets and lady-fingers. She approached the two
boys, and after staring fiercely at the intruder, she turned to the
seated boy. 'Spit on him, Jimmie,' she said.

The boy in the corduroy breeches stepped back, intimidated
by this reception. 'What wud he want tae spit on me fur,' he
protested, 'sure I never did ye ony harm?' Then with an in-
gratiating smile he continued, 'What are ye tied like that fur,
wee lad?'

The boy still remained with his eyes on the ground, his
cheeks perhaps a shade darker, the white stones motionless on
the grass. The little girl put her foot with its square-toed boot in
the crotch of a bush and swung her knee. 'It's because he wet
the bed!' she said.

The boy in the corduroy breeches gave an incredulous 'heh!'
'Jimmie,' the girl appealed, 'didn't Gramma tether ye fur
wettin' the bed?'

'Ye think ye're quare an' funny, wee girl,' said the boy in the
corduroy breeches. For answer the girl threw back her head,
pursed her lips, and spat violently in the direction of the
sceptic. Her expectoration was more violent than scientific, for
all that appeared was a fine spray which fell through the warm
air on the bended head of her brother.

For the first time the boy on the ground spoke. 'Girls are no
good of spitters,' he said, wiping his cheek. At this treachery
his sister gave an indignant cry, and raising her foot delivered
him a solid kick on the haunch, then turned and fled down the
loanen, her short serge skirt tearing at the seeding grass.

The boy on the ground nursed his leg, gazing after the fleeing
figure of his sister. 'Wull ye help me tae catch her?' he asked the
other. 'I wull that,' answered the boy in the corduroy breeches.
'We'll throw her in the linthole,' said the boy on the ground.
'Ach, no,' said the other, 'sure we micht drownd her.'

Jimmie got up, removed the collar from his ankle, pulled up his stockings and nodding to the boy in the breeches, set off after his sister. He moved with a roll, slow but strong, his heavy bottom jutting as he ran. The other boy was lighter and swifter, accelerating where the grass was thin, running close on the other's heels.

At a gap in the hedge Jimmie stopped. 'There she is,' he said, 'crossin' owr the bog meadow. Go you roun' by the tap an' kep her till I catch her.' The other boy nodded and jumped over into the field. He had run a few paces when Jimmie called him back. 'Hi, boy, what dae they call ye?'

'Francie McCoy.'

'I'm Jimmie Orr an' her name's Nannie Orr. She's my sister. Now you kep her in frae the tap.'

In a few minutes they had so overhauled and surrounded the little girl that she retreated to the top of a fallen yellow hay-rick where she stood swaying precariously, a sod in each hand, shouting defiance. With a wild whuroo her brother rushed the stronghold, catching an ill-aimed missile as he ran, and gaining the top flung himself down at her feet with a laugh, rolling over on his back with his face to the sun. Francie dropped his outstretched arms, greatly relieved that he had not actually to grapple with the defiant young termagant. He approached the rick as Jimmie invitingly patted the warm straw. 'Wur ye in earnest aboot throwin' her in the linthole?' he asked.

Jimmie threw back his head and laughed. 'Ach, I wus only jokin'.' He stretched up to stroke his sister's tumbled fair hair as she knelt between the boys. 'Sure I wudn't throw Nannie in the hole fur ony money.' Nannie's head bent to her brother's caressing, then straightening up she said to Francie with pointed emphasis, 'We cud throw you in the hole.'

Suddenly Jimmie slipped down to the sharp elastic stubble. 'Come on, we'll mak bows an' arris an' hunt!' Although Francie and the sister were but a few feet away, he bellowed his words, a crimson figure against the ashy stubble, waving his arm imperiously like a commander rallying a cavalry charge.

The golden wands swayed and fell as a muddy heel or strong fingers tore at them close to the water's surface. Jimmie snapped the frond heads and tossed them to Nannie. Francie and he notched the ends and strung them, then with blackhead reeds as arrows they went hunting.

But the osiers were young and green and full of sap, and after a pull or two they straightened slowly like a tired goat's leg and the reed slithered harmlessly over the grass. 'D'ye know what my Granpa says?' said Jimmie, throwing his bow on the ground, 'he says if you tuk a good ashplant there, an' put it in the chimley tae dry, and then strung it wi' a thong, ye cud drive a sally rod through a byre dure wi' it.'

'Aye, an' maybe kill a baste,' said Francie laughing.

A look of exasperation came on Jimmie's face. 'Ye're a quare silly wee fella, Francis. Sure ye'd tak the bastes out before ye'd dae ony firin'.'

'D'ye go tae ony school, Francie McCoy?' asked Nannie.

'Nane aya, but I'm goin' after the harvest.'

'D'ye think ye'll be goin' tae Ballyilveen School where ould Master Rankin is?'

'Ma father wants me tae go tae a town school.'

The Orrs lay back on their elbows and looked at him. Idly Francie picked up one of the discarded bows, unstrung it and cast it along the grass. Immediately Jimmie was on his feet. 'Spears is just as good as arris. We'll go huntin' wi' spears.' 'We'll go,' said Nannie in a thrilled whisper, 'tae Master Rankin's diamon' and hunt his goat.'

Admiration, affection and excitement passed over Jimmie's face as he gazed at his sister. 'Nannie,' he said, 'ye're a quare wee girl.' Then he set off across the field, thrashing his thigh with an osier, in search of Master Rankin's goat.

They came on the goat cropping quietly under the lea of the hedge which ran around the little diamond-shaped field. Every few seconds she would shake her bearded head free from the clegs and flies which sipped at the rims of her old eyes. 'Watch!' breathed Jimmie. His wand sped through the hedge, bounced on the razor-like spine of the goat and ricocheted into the field. The goat jumped with a clatter of its tethering-chain, her head lowered to the hedge. At the same time a man in soiled riding breeches and unbuttoned waistcoat sprang on top of the dyke, clutching the bushes with one hand to steady himself and brandishing a billhook in the other. 'G'wan, ye wee whelps ye!' he shouted. 'Ah, it's you, Jimmie Orr, I'll teach you to maltreat a poor beast of a goat!' He sprang over the hedge and stooping down picked up a stone and flung it after the fleeing children. He hitched, as a countryman does, from the waist, and the missile hummed over Francie's head like an angry bee.

'It was oul' Rankin brerdin' his hedge,' gasped Jimmie as they breasted the steep slope of the grazing field. The man continued to shout threats after them, his last shot reaching their ears as they disappeared over the slope, 'I'll tell your Grandma you're skiltin' the fields with a papish, my bold Jimmie Orr!'

They reached the little loanen, shadows gathered in the nooks of its old gnarled hedges, the insect sounds dissolved and gone in the cool evening air. Jimmie squatted down and searched in the grass for his white stones. Nannie shivered, and said she was going to bring in the ducks. 'Can I come too?' asked Fancie. She looked at him coldly and passed by without reply. Francie hung round watching Jimmie as he scrubbed a blood-spangled knee with spittle and a docken leaf. At last he ostentatiously buttoned his jacket, 'So long, Jimmie,' he said. 'So long, wee fella,' answered Jimmie without raising his head.

A shrill cry halted Francie in his path. Nannie had climbed on the farm-close gate, a finger pointed at the distant Francie. She lowered her voice when she saw her brother's head bobbing up the loanen hedge. 'Tell that wee fella to come over an' play the morra,' she said. Francie heard and waved his arm in reply. 'I wull, Nannie, I wull!' he shouted. Then he turned and rushed down the dusky loanen, kicking madly at the dew-heavy grass in his delight.

SAM HANNA BELL was born in Glasgow in 1909 of Irish parents but on the death of his father came 'home' to Co. Down. After an almost American career of many jobs he joined the BBC in Belfast in 1945 and was Senior Features Producer till 1969. His outstanding novel, *December Bride* (1951) recently republished has a Hardean profundity and wildness and conveys as the work of no writer since Shan F. Bullock does the life of rural Protestant Ulster, with its hard work, frugality, self-sufficiency and watchfulness. Other novels about the North are *The Hollow Ball* (1961) and *A Man Flourishing* (1973). His interest in Ulster folkways is continuous as his book *Erin's Orange Lily* (1956) shows. He is an authority on the Ulster theatre and has written the standard book on the subject, *The Theatre in Ulster* (1972). His most recent publication *Within Our Province* is a compilation from many sources of life in Ulster for the last three centuries. 'Summer Loanen' was the first story he had published and became the title for his first book, a collection of short stories. The Ulster word 'loanen' is equivalent to 'boreen'.

SUMMER LOANEN   *Sam Hanna Bell*   *December 1941*

LONDON LIONS

By PATRICK CAMPBELL

I GOT round to Lord Donegall about eleven-thirty. Up till then I had been squeezing the juice out of David Grey, Cyril Connolly and Sean MacEntee. Lord Donegall was down at the far end of the room with Erskine Childers, groping a little in the Celtic twilight. I placed myself between them and the refreshment counter, on the chance that this would provide an opportunity to cut off one or the other before many minutes had passed. Lord Donegall made the first break. I poured, consolidating the gain.

'Speak to me, Lord Donegall,' I said, about mid-way, 'of Europe tense upon the brink of war.'

Now, what I wanted was intimate fact, vivid glimpses of the captains and the kings at lunch, the weight of Goering's cigar-case, and Mussolini's face after he has jumped over a row of bayonets. The only personal details we get about the war are from the *Irish Times,* and they only say that Comrade Joe is, after all, a realist. They also say that Herr Hitler is, after all, a realist, so it may be more of a filler than a genuine revelation.

Lord Donegall spoke for some time about Europe tense upon the brink of war, but long before the end I could see it was a frost. No give. Merely general descriptive stuff without an indiscretion. But he did say one thing that I remembered. He said: 'So I popped down in my plane to see jolly old Zog,' and that was the last straw. At no time, and in no place, is King Zog, black-eyed bandit of the mountains, lord of the tribesmen, and brother to as queer a pack of sisters as ever trod this earth, merely 'jolly old Zog'. And Lord Donegall should know it.

But perhaps I tried him too high. Lord Donegall is, after all, a celebrity, and you never get a thing out of them. I say it quite simply. You never get a thing out of a celebrity. Not a sausage.

Look at Lord Beaverbrook. Lord Beaverbrook and I — allowing for the difference in altitudes — worked shoulder to shoulder and cheek by jowl for one hundred and eighty-six days and nights. He would ring me up at eight in the morning, announcing the dawn of another day, and urging speed to the plough. In my absence he would leave messages with the landlady — 'Lord Beaverbrook wishes to know where you are.' The maid even came in on it at the end, and would give me the latest with no trace of excitement. Lord Beaverbrook became a commonplace round our house... 'He was on again,' and so forth.

This hand-in-glove work suggested that we were on the verge of an unusual intimacy. Daily I expected the summons to move in. I could see us in the cool of the evening down at Cherkley after dinner, me with an old brandy and Lord Beaverbrook with his asthma lozenges, just two good friends working towards a common aim.

What happened? Punctually at the end of six months Lord Beaverbrook and I parted company, and that by remote control. A secretary, authorised to express no words of sorrow or farewell, slipped me the final envelope in a back room at the *Evening Standard*. I left in a rage.

I should make myself plain. This outburst of temper was caused not by the loss of the job — at the time of the severance I was writing a series of articles entitled, 'Great Deeds that Won Our Crown Colonies' — but by a knowledge of the difficulties that now lay before me. What in the name of God was I going to say about Lord Beaverbrook? Cheek by jowl for twenty-four weeks, and a stock of anecdote barely sufficient to hold a small table in Mitchell's. A nice outcome.

The blow fell almost at once. Shortly after my return to Dublin, Mr. MacEntee asked me what Lord Beaverbrook thought about Ireland. I struggled with my recollections for some minutes in almost complete silence. I remember a light beading of perspiration even appeared upon my forehead. But in the end I had to admit that I could not recall Lord Beaver-

brook ever actually referring to the subject of Ireland in my
presence.

The following are the things that I *do* remember about Lord
Beaverbrook. It's a rotten beginning to 'Glimpses of the Great,'
but I cannot bother about setting the stage. Get it out and get
it over, is my motto.

The first anecdote is called 'Lord Beaverbrook and Lord
Forbes,' a good title with upper-class ring.

One day I went into Lord Beaverbrook's study in Stornoway
House. Lord Forbes was there, leaning upon the mantelpiece.
Lord Beaverbrook said to Lord Forbes as I entered: 'Go to
Maascow, write whaat they're thinking, take my airplane.'
Incomparably the worst part of this anecdote is that fact that
that is the end. There is no more to it, just a short anecdote
about Lord Beaverbrook and Lord Forbes. I usually bump it
out by saying something about Lord Beaverbrook's Canadian
accent, and passing from there to his liking for semi-biblical
talk.

'Praasecute your enquiries diligently,' he will say, 'until
you reach the end.' And in reproof: 'Garner the craaps more
swiftly, lest you no laanger find yourself amid the harvesters in
the field.' There is no man, woman or child in the *Daily Express*
offices who cannot imitate this accent to the life.

The second anecdote is called 'Lord Beaverbrook on his Road
To Waterloo'.

One day I went into Lord Beaverbrook's study in Stornoway
House. Lord Forbes was not leaning upon the mantelpiece.
Lord Beaverbrook said to me: 'Come to Waterloo'.
Immediately, on principle, I asked him what for. At times he
would be a shade abrupt. Lord Beaverbrook did not raise his
head from the lunch-time *Standard*. 'Whaat's it to you?' he
asked. I checked myself in time. We did not speak again until
we were under the Admiralty Arch.

'Your grandfather was a great man,' said Lord Beaverbrook,
making fairly plain what it had cost him not to begin with 'at
any rate'.

I replied that my grandfather had no artistic sensibilities.
Lord Beaverbrook at once asked me what I meant. I could not
answer. We completed the rest of the drive in silence.

We arrived at Waterloo. Lord Beaverbrook got out of the
Rolls. At that moment a taxi dashed up behind us and dis-

gorged a flood of secretaries, butlers, note-takers and other
hangers-on. They all began to speak at once. After several
moments Lord Beaverbrook and I got the gist of it. It seemed
that his Lordship was supposed to be going to Victoria, and not,
as we previously had supposed, to Waterloo. Lord Beaverbrook
stepped back into the car, and slammed the door firmly behind
him. The car immediately drove off, leaving me standing on
the pavement.

There, then, is the sum total of my Beaverbrook material,
a thin enough yield in all conscience. Two anecdotes and a
short descriptive passage after one hundred and eighty-six days
of close association.

But there is even worse to come. Some time after I ceased to
operate in Fleet Street I was invited to play cricket for charity
at a private house in Regent's Park. The match was billed as
'The Authors' versus 'The Actresses'. I was down to play for
the former, though even this biologically sound arrangement
became confused before the end. I rode out to Regent's Park in
a mood of optimism and forgiveness. The events of the afternoon would more than compensate me, I felt, for the six barren
months with the Imp.

Straight off I was shown into a changing-room that contained the half-clad persons of C. S. Forester and Louis
MacNeice. A little later A. G. Macdonell looked in. Somebody
said that H. G. Wells was on his way.

'Fine afternoon,' I said happily to Alec Waugh, as we strolled
down the steps of the house.

The match began. Four hours later the wind was a little
colder, and there were rather fewer spectators, but otherwise
nothing had happened. I stood at the west end of the pitch
near the bushes, even now unable to realise the extent of the
disaster. For the past twenty minutes Louis MacNeice had been
lifting Miss Swinburne's bowling high above my head into the
dense and cat-ridden patch of foliage behind my back. I
retrieved the ball while the rest of them chatted of Books and
the Stage at the other end.

I reviewed my intimate and significant details. Isabel Jeans
got herself run out by a young actress in interesting shorts. And
what happened? Miss Jeans quietly went home, admittedly
vexed, but with never a hair pulled, nor a fair young cheek
laid open. All day long Shane Leslie ran about in a small and

pot-like schoolboy's cap, shouting and being funny, and nobody tripped him up.

There was one moment that looked like the dawn of better things. A. P. Herbert came out to bowl with a box of garden produce, and sent down a shower of mixed vegetables with a quite delightful *élan*. Seeing Shane Leslie looking for a battered grape in the long grass was very, very good. But it came to nothing. They took Herbert off as he was levering a marrow out of his box, and put on Forester with a conservative Sorbo.

It was like that all along the line. These Lions would come to the very edge of their Big Scene, and then fritter the whole thing away as the very curtain went up.

The match came to an end amid some unpleasantness. Louis MacNeice, forgetting poetic fancy in the shame of a three innings defeat, was lashing about him like a blacksmith. What had begun as a divertissement now became practically war to the knife. At first the more elderly and fantastically garbed actresses handled the bowling, flapping the ball from end to end with many a charming *moue* at their own delicious, if calculated, incompetence, but now they were putting on the hard stuff, athletic young girls in workmanlike tennis dresses, but lately down from Girton. These Junos worked on MacNeice with everything from body-line to walking across the pitch as he was about to play. But the poet remained impregnable, scoring freely all round the wicket with a child's toy bat. In the end Priestley had to do a good deal of bluff smoothing over in his best-hearted manner. Everybody fell for it however in the most milk and water manner, and we parted company politely.

After that I came back to Dublin for good. For a week or so I had some success in the lower-class bars, but the scantiness of the material was all too obvious. People would pause for a moment as they heard me mention Lord Beaverbrook or Godfrey Winn, and then pass on to some deeper well. By the end of the month I was desperate. And then, gradually, by imperceptible stages, the situation began to ease. Do you know what was happening? Very, very slightly I was beginning to toy with the truth. Here a little, there a little I started to present events that had never, in strict fact, actually taken place. There would be a small concession to reality in the framework of the story, but that was all. The rest would be invention, pure and unashamed.

'Beachcomber turned up at this Authors' and Actresses' cricket match slightly the worse for drink. He played in his braces and bare feet, using his attache case for a bat. Immediately upon the conclusion of his innings he flung on his shoes, snatched his coat, and fled away down the avenue crying: "A pint — a pint! Strabismus for a pint!".'

That kind of thing. Gifty, with a little practice and the essential framework.

'Now and then I used to go down and stay with Beaverbrook for the week-end at Cherkley. Every Sunday morning we would go out to the swimming pool, Beaverbrook dressed for the sport, me with a notebook and pencil. Beaverbrook would jump in at the deep end feet first, holding his nose, and begin swimming about under water. Every time he would break surface some fresh instruction would emerge, together with about a pint of water. The fresh instruction I conveyed to the pages of the notebook. In this way we laboured without cessation.'

And did I labour without cessation upon the edges of the Cherkley pool? Not on your life I didn't, but George Malcolm Thomson and Peter Howard did, and that was all that I wanted to know. There are now no limits to my life with the great.

'I once drove Helen Wills to Renvyle. You remember the time she was over here at Fitzwilliam? Well, the same Wills thought of nothing but her tennis. It was tennis all the way with that one. Do you know, we'd barely got as far as Lucan before she was asking me not to drive so fast — "because all this scenery rushing past my eye upsets my timing!" What a woman! What a racquet!' (By the Renvyle connection it must have been Gogarty who met Helen Wills. It was certain wasn't me.)

'One night I was up at Priestley's. The usual gang was there, Victor Gollancz, Rose Macaulay, Robert Lynd, Norman Collins, David Cecil and the rest. Rose drove me out, talking all the time, as is the way with her, and driving mostly with one wheel on the pavement. I was a little bored, Cecil had just been telling me about how he was redecorating his bathroom, so I strolled over to the drink table. Now there was a curious domestic custom in the Priestley house by which whiskies were always poured out and left on a large tray, ready for the guests to add soda or water as they wished. One never saw the bottle.

As I mixed two or three tumblerfuls together I noticed a morose-looking man watching me. His hair was iron grey, he wore a pair of American glasses. By his side stood a tall, beautiful brunette. A sudden memory flashed upon me. James Thurber! James Thurber, by all his life and hard times. "Hi, Thurber," I said, carelessly. Well, in no time at all we were hitting it up like anything. The tall brunette turned out to be Jim's wife, and they were both fed up with the conventionally-minded literati. I remember we finished up hours later at Smokey's giving imitations in turn of the conventionally-minded literati, and David Cecil painting a bathroom. Talk about the night the bed fell on father!'

The essence of this method is its minute yet undeniable foundation in fact. Anybody who has been to the Priestley house will recognise the item about the whiskies poured out; anybody who has been in a motor-car with Miss Macaulay must also have been on the pavement. But unless they have also been there at the same time as myself they can provide no further check. And do I handpick my audience?

Nothing but sheer physical exhaustion can limit my repertoire. That − and one other little matter. I could go on all night about the time that Prince Chavchavadze played the piano so loudly that the pictures fell off the walls, about the duet I sang with John McCormack; and about what I said when Mrs. Robeson began to boss my poor friend Paul. All night, I say, if it was not for this one other little matter.

This one other little matter is a feeling that all my not be well with my mind. The unhappy truth is that I no longer seem to be able to make any worth-while distinction between fact and fiction. That is to say that I can no longer tell for certain if any of the events which I retail did, in fact, occur. To this day I cannot say if I have ever met Count John McCormack; I preserve an open mind about my friendship with Florence Desmond and Schnozzle Durante.

Does it portend a canvas-waistcoat, with sleeves made fast behind the back? Is my bed already turned down at the Grange?

PATRICK CAMPBELL, 3rd Baron Glenavy, was born in Dublin in 1913, educated at Rossall and Oxford and also in Paris and Germany. At the beginning of the Emergency he served in the Irish Navy and from

1944 to 1947 three even more exhausting and hilarious years on *The Irish Times* under Smyllie. He has been a humorous columnist ever since, commenting in a gentle way upon the follies of human nature, particularly his own. A slight speech impediment he turned into a badge of personality. This and his own limpid nature have made him a much-loved TV personality. Of many books of very funny pieces which he has published, *A Short Trot with a Cultured Mind* (1952) is perhaps his best and most appropriate title. His weekly column in *The Sunday Times* now in its eighteenth splendid year shows no sign of flagging. His account of his Dublin adventures when he was the ornament of Westmoreland Street are to be found in *My Life and Easy Times* (1967). His most recent book, *Thirty-Five Years on the Job* is in print in paperback. He has lived in the south of France for sixteen years, that is when he is not calling Frank Muir's bluff.

LONDON LIONS or:
You might as well stay in Dublin   *Patrick Campbell*   *March 1942*

A SERVANT GIRL
TO HER FAITHLESS LOVER

By ROBERT GREACEN

To you, holding in spent hands all seasons memories,
Bush and briar, thorn and thistle and tree,
I send my love all wrapped and sealed
With the tense, white paper of my sentiment.
Crying in the various nights of muffled rain
(O live lead lash on the window-sill)
For you are frozen and alien from my side,
I send my freshness and my ardour.
To you, folding on hard palms all seasons' memories,
Gorse and foxglove, berry and subtle humming bee,
I post my love all crumpled and sealed
With the gum of lips you stormed to starve.

ROBERT GREACEN was born in Derry in 1920 and is now a teacher in London where he has lived since 1948. The account of his early life in the North is given in *Even Without Irene* (1969) which also recounts with marvellous tenderness and humour the end of a teenage love-affair. He has published much poetry, the most recent volume, *A Garland for Captain Fox,* appearing in Dublin in 1975. He is a regular reviewer for *The Irish Press.* This poem is the only one of his early pieces that he cares to have preserved.

A SERVANT GIRL TO HER FAITHLESS LOVER
Robert Greacen   *April 1942*

I BECOME A BORSTAL BOY

By BRENDAN BEHAN

I AWOKE on the morning of the 7th February, 1940, with a feeling of despondency. I'd had a restless night and fell asleep only to be awakened an hour later by the bell that roused myself and 1,253 other prisoners in Walton Jail.

As I awoke the thought that had lain heavily with me through the night realised itself into words — 'If they carry it out'. Just then I heard the shout 'Right, all doors open. Slop out'. They will die in two and a quarter hours.

Then another thought followed into my mind. 'I might go down to Assizes to-day'. But I had said that every day since January 29, when I had been informed at the Committal Court that commission day for Liverpool Winter Assizes Court was six weeks off.

I rose and washed myself and settled myself to wait for the rattling of keys and opening of doors that would indicate that my breakfast was on its way. After breakfast I heard the call, 'Right, R.C's. Parade for Ash Wednesday Service,' and when the other Catholic juvenile offenders of C wing had been marched away to chapel my cell door was opened and I was escorted there in solitary state. I went to my usual place

between Ned, a Royal Engineer from Carlow, awaiting trial for
housebreaking, and Gerry, a Monaghan lad of Republican ideas
and of many convictions. A whispered conversation ensued.

'Brendan,' Gerry whispered, 'they died two minutes ago.'

Down the long rows of brown-clad remands and in the convicted pews where the blue uniform of the Borstal Boys
contrasted with the grey slops of the penal servitude one could
see on every Irish face the imprint of the tragedy that had been
enacted that morning in another prison and that was to every
Irishman present a personal sorrow. Ned and Gerry nodded to
me. 'O.K., Brendan, say the word.'

I stood up in my pew and raised my hand in the signal we
had agreed upon the previous Sunday.

'Irishmen, attention!'

A rigid silence gripped the chapel. The warders stood
bewildered. No doubt many of them thought it was a special
ceremony of the Church in which the congregation took part.
One young warder fingered his baton nervously.

'Irishmen, attention!'

Ned and Gerry were already on their feet.

'We will recite the *De Profundis* for the repose of the souls
of our countrymen who gave their lives for Ireland this morning
in Birmingham Jail.'

Gerry (who knew it) began. 'Out of the depths have I cried
to thee, O Lord...' Back down the serried rows came the
response. 'Lord hear my voice.' An old Corkman serving seven
years for manslaughter was standing in the back rows reserved
for elderly preventative detentions. In front of him was a big
Mayo lad awaiting transfer to Parkhurst or Dartmoor. 'And let
my cry come unto thee...'

Suddenly the Principal Officer appeared to regain his com-
posure. He shouted orders. 'Remove Lawlor and Behan to their
cells. Sit down the rest of you. Damn you! Silence!'

Soon I was struggling as two warders grabbed me. Ned, the
big Carlow soldier was fighting madly. Gerry's head went down
amid the impact of batons. The old Corkman I last saw as they
removing him, a scarlet gash showing vividly against his white
hair. Raising my head I saw a baton poised ready to strike. I
croushed, tensing myself for the blow, but it never came: the
P.O.'s. voice cut in clear above the din. 'Don't strike Behan!
He's for court to-day.'

I was removed to my cell and told that I was damned lucky that I was being discharged that day as otherwise I would have been reported to the Governor with the others and have got No. 1 (bread and water) 'to cool me off'.

Some hours later my door was opened and I heard the 'away' call: 'Right, two away for Liverpool Assizes'. I was one: the other was an alleged murderer whose trial was reaching its concluding stages. I was taken alone, however, to the reception room. There I saw six men standing in line and a seventh standing alone by the desk. He must be the alleged murderer. He smiled pleasantly and wished me 'good morning'.

I was motioned into one of a row of cubicles and told to undress and have a bath. Having bathed I returned to my cubicle and dressed. I had been wearing prison clothes, as my own had been removed for examination and analysis by Home Office experts. With what a thrill of pleasure I now put my hands in my trousers pockets! I was next called out to sign for the money and sundries that I had had in my possession when arrested.

'It's a waste of time with you, Paddy, doing all this bloody signing. We all know damn well you'll be back to start your twenty years!'

The warder winked at one of the escorts.

'What d'you reckon you'll get, Paddy? 'Anged, drawn and quartered, or just plain 'anging?'

'Benefit of the Probation Act and ten shillings out of the Poor Box to mend my boots,' I replied.

'Yes, if you can slip that stuff over old Mr. Justice Whosis, all about you bein' only sixteen years of age and so on! What *is* your age, Paddy – straight-up – between what's present like.'

'I was born the ninth of February, nineteen twenty-three.'

'Yes? I bet you was sixteen when Charley Peace was president of the Everton Valley Band of 'Ope. Oh, well! Argue it out between yourself and Mr. Justice Who-is-it.'

And I stood aside.

'Here's the other one for Assizes, Jack!' shouted the second escort. 'O.K., Crippen! Come along.' We went along. Instead of going in the Black Maria we travelled to the city in a small police car. I took stock of my companion and thought that despite the ordeal of a four days' murder-trial he appeared extraordinarily calm. He inquired where I was from and seemed

surprised when I told him the nature of my offence. I was
wondering in what form to put my own question, for it seemed
rude to ask 'Who did you kill?' At last I found a more delicate
formula. 'Who was the deceased concerned with your case?'

'Oh!' he answered, 'my wife was found about three months
ago with her head battered in,' quite as if it happened by act
of God. 'As we had quarrelled some days before it was not
unnatural for the authorities to charge me. But, of course, I
shall be acquitted.'

He spoke with such evident sincerity that when I read later
an account of his execution I wondered if he had been guilty
after all.

My cell at George's Hall was quite unlike those I had known
in either prison or police-station. It had a barred door similar
to the prison scenes in an American film. On the walls were the
usual inscriptions. 'J.S. stole a lady's watch to keep it safe.
3 years P.S. 15-4-35.' In addition were inscriptions by Irishmen
who had been sentenced at the previous Assizes. 'We ask no
quarter – we seek no compromise. Stephen Casey.' Steve had
been acquitted and was now home in his native Meath. 'Jim
Flynn, 5 years. P.S. Dublin Brigade.' Jim was a lad from
Ringsend and had been a particular friend of mine. He was in
Maidstone. 'Jerry Robinson. Operations Officer. South Wales.
15 years.' They had dealt with him rather severely, probably on
account of his nationality: he was an Englishman.

I scratched my own inscription, a quotation from Pearse:
'We cannot be beaten because the cause we serve enshrines
the soul of Ireland.' Under it I wrote my name and left a space
for my sentence. The P.O. brought some coffee and bully-
beef sandwiches. The alleged murderer had his food sent in by
relatives. He asked me if I would like some banana sandwiches.

'Take the lot, son. It'll be a long time before you'll get the
taste of skilly out of your mouth.'

Amid a fanfare of trumpets the judge entered and seated
himself. Then the clerk, magnificently arrayed in what appeared
to be a red hunting jacket, began the list of alleged offences
that constituted the bone of contention between the King and
myself. I refused to plead and the prosecuting counsel, dressed
in his officer's uniform, began his case. He spoke quite without
passion, called his witnesses and in about two hours the case
was nearly settled. I had expected a jury of twelve, but could

only count eight, including three women. I wondered if any of them were annoyed with me for upsetting the routine of a shop or office. A young man of about eighteen sitting beside the judge smiled and winked at me in a comradely fashion. When the jury had returned their verdict, which they did without retiring, the Judge asked if I had anything to say before he passed sentence. I proceeded to speak and he interrupted me and told me that what I was saying wasn't likely to induce him to give me a light sentence. However, I had learnt that speech off by heart and thought it rather good and I did not intend to be sentenced without getting the worth of my money, so I told him that if it was all the same to him I would prefer to continue. When I had concluded he began himself by saying that he felt that the laws regarding the sentencing of juvenile offenders were inadequate to deal with a case like this. He made a fine speech in which he showed an acquaintance with Synge and concluded by saying that unfortunately the aforesaid laws regarding juvenile offenders did not allow him to give me the fourteen years' penal servitude which he remarked (entirely without malice) I deserved. The only sentence he could give me there was three years' Borstal detention.

As I passed down my murderer friend was on his way to the dock. I shook hands with him and wished him luck. He smiled confidently, waved his hands and shouted, 'Good-bye.' 'I hope so,' I murmured, 'for your sake.' Two and a half hours later he was removed prostrate from the dock and left in a cell next door to me. On the return journey we spoke little and even the escort conversed in subdued tones. It was like going to a funeral. As we parted finally he smiled wanly as he looked me straight in the face. 'Good luck, Paddy.'

'Right, one away Borstal landing Y.P. wing,' and in a softer tone: 'one away to D 2 14.' (The number of the condemned cell.)

As I lay in bed I calculated, as hundreds must have done in the same place, 'How soon will I get out?' I worked it out that with a bit of remission I would be released in January, 1942. I settled down for sleep. Somewhere on Merseyside a church bell rang out. It was nine o'clock...

BRENDAN BEHAN was born in Dublin in 1923 and died there in

1964. He had for some years a reputation as a writer of great promise among a fairly narrow circle in Dublin but after the English success of his prison play, *The Quare Fellow* in 1956 he became public property. His meteoric rise included the publication of *Borstal Boy* (1958) a brilliant account of his three year confinement for IRA offences and the play *The Hostage* (1959) which almost became a revue when it was 'adapted' by Joan Littlewood and her Theatre Workshop. Whatever effect, good or bad, producers may have had upon the plays *Borstal Boy* is Behan's own and is likely to remain his best regarded work and his finest memorial. This early sketch for that book was written for *The Bell* when Behan was nineteen; it shows his humour, capacity for setting a scene and conveying the idiosyncracy of character and total lack of self-pity.

I BECOME A BORSTAL BOY   Brendan Behan   *June 1942*

PEADAR O'DONNELL

By JOHN HEWITT

I remember walking through the August twilight
along the narrow lane from house to house
the boys still playing hurley loud and shouting
and a black calf that turned with mournful cry.

It seemed the long way round that we had taken
over a rough ground higher than the bog.
Three fields away white foam was on the breakers.
Storm's opposition made us both dog-tired.

Then darkness came and window after window
Held out its yellow candle. We went on
slow pacing now and painfully admonished
by gulls that cried above the water's din.

We reached the three small houses and the gate
that faced them where the drive turned to the right.
It was too late to make a call we argued;
there was no blink of light in any room.

But half-way down the drive we saw the writer
still working in the garden with his wife.
I shouted and he straightened up to answer
And in the gloom his fine head glimmered white.

JOHN HEWITT was born in Belfast in 1907 and graduated from Queen's with an MA, his thesis being on nineteenth-century Ulster poets. At the age of 23 he joined the staff of the Belfast museum and Art Gallery and became Deputy Director by 1957 when he was appointed Art Director of the Herbert Art Gallery and Museum in Coventry. He returned to Belfast in 1970 and is at present writer in residence at Queen's University. He has a considerable reputation as art critic and historian and is undoubtedly one of Ulster's finest poets. His work has done much to help the northern Protestant to come to some accommodation with his own past and his position with regard to the other tradition.

PEADAR O'DONNELL   *John Hewitt*   *July 1942*

THE FROST WAS HARD
By MAURICE JAMES CRAIG

The frost was hard those days, the sunlight clean
Each morning on the snow, and every night
Our footsteps rang like iron on the road
As, walking homeward through the misty air,
We kept the mist of breath about us. You
Remember still, thawing the frozen pipes
With cans of boiling water?

That frost was hard for you and me; but now
The long sobs of the dying afternoon
Are caught and choked in autumn's throat. The leaves,
Made fools of by the black heart of the wind,
Skelter along the pathways. In the west
The flickering furnace glows more cold, and there
Beyond the mountains desolately stretch
The bitter marshes under the empty sky.

Where can we find the water now, to thaw
These frozen seas of blood, that superfused
With blood fresh-flowing, congeal about the heart?
The generous impulse in the arteries
That circulate between us, has not flagged
On either side. For that and all it means
My gratitude is inarticulate
And best employed to keep those channels free
Through all the darkness of this winter night.

MAURICE JAMES CRAIG was born in Belfast in 1919. His poetry was printed in *The Bell* and other journals and printed in two volumes, *Black Swans* (1941) and *Some Way for Reason* (1948). He is best known as the biographer of the Earl of Charlemont in *The Volunteer Earl* (1948) and as Dublin's historian with *Dublin City Churches* (1948) and *Dublin 1600-1800* (1952); he also wrote an account of Irish Bookbinding in 1954. From 1952 to 1970 he was employed in England by the Ministry of Works as Inspector of Ancient Monuments. Since his return to Dublin in 1970 he has written the commentary to Kieran Hickey's film about one of Ireland's truly noble institutions, *Portrait of a Library.* In 1977 he published *Classic Irish Houses of the Middle Size.* In Ulster he is cherished for his pasquinade 'May the Lord in His Mercy Look Down on Belfast'. He lives in south Dublin.

THE FROST WAS HARD   Maurice J. Craig   *December 1942*

AN ARCH PURPLE PAST
By CAMPBELL BARTON

A T one period of my life I used to pray once a month for Roman Catholics. I never bothered to ask myself whether I was praying for the Roman Catholic Church at large or only for Irish Roman Catholics, and, anyway, it did not seem to me that my prayers would do either of them any good, anyway. Those were the days when I belonged to an Orange Lodge, days when the little ornaments on a sash meant something to me – the three-runged ladder, the six-pointed star and all the rest. To-day, I am sorry to say, their significance is hazy. I am sorry, because my memory seems to be going. For all the implications of the Arch Purple Degree were impressed upon my mind and my body somewhat painfully and sometimes brutally by a Chapter of Belfast bakers, some of whom were not sober enough to lend dignity to the proceedings. Such was the nature of the ordeal that any candidate who had a physical or organic failing, like a dickery heart, watched the rough and tumble from a side seat.

The ceremonies of the Arch Purple Chapter had been preceded by an Orange Lodge meeting, and between the two there had been a wild scatter from Clifton Street to the nearest public houses in Carlisle Circus, so that a great deal of time was lost trying to assemble a quorum for the opening of the Chapter. This had a serious digestive sequel. It was the time of murder and riot euphemistically known as 'The Troubles', and there was a curfew in force, with the result that only twenty minutes remained for the supper which followed the meetings. Sweet biscuits and cheese were eaten as fast as the jaws could work, and bottles of stout were drunk as fast as the stewards could pull them. I remember having a glass to my lips and a hand outstretched for the next bottle.

There are no secrets in the Orange Order and none in the Purple Order, apart from the entrance word, which is changed annually. The secret signs, words and half-words are preserved in the Arch Purple Chapters, but the only persons I ever saw using the signs or heard mentioning the words and half-words were country farm boys who were not Orangemen at all. The one thing that struck me as important in the Degree was a sign and series of words which were supposed to be used when one was in imminent peril of losing one's life, whereupon any Orangeman who heard was expected to come to the rescue immediately. I never could remember either the sign or the words, and the only Orangeman that I subsequently asked about them could not remember either. So much for the secrets of the Orange or any other Order — Buffs, Elks, Knights or K.K.K. Secrets, ritual and regalia are part of the entertainment for which the annual or monthly subscription is paid. So strong is the youthful strain in most of us that, when a Lodge gets careless about the mumbo-jumbo, its membership tends to decrease. Certain churches probably have had the same experience.

I do remember that on my way home from Clifton Street on the night of my initiation, being in possession of a curfew permit, I made two calls. The first was to the Nightworkers' Social Club, all trace of which now has been effaced, a bomb from the *Luftwaffe* having accomplished what various antisocial Head Constables failed to do in the past. Having drunk there more leisurely, I made the second call, to my lady love. She charged me, correctly, with having drink taken, and, again correctly, with the intention of taking some more from the bottles which protruded from my jacket pockets. The night's activities collectively had made some impression upon me, for with a show of emotion I exclaimed: 'If you had been through what I have been through, *you* would have taken a drink.' To which the lady love replied with a word that was neither decent nor ambiguous and slammed the door.

Apart from one occasion, when a deputation tried to enlist the support of my brethren for a political, or semi-political, object, the most important thing I ever heard discussed in an Orange Lodge was the arrangements for the annual dinner. There was quite a lively discussion, however, on the question of whether we should carry our new banner to 'the Field' or employ four hirelings to save our muscles. The carrying of a banner for even half-an-hour is hard work, and we finally decided to engage some hefty labouring men to bear the responsibility, the poles, and the picture of William III.

Incidentally, in all my associations with the Orange Order, I never once heard the Pope mentioned. If ever you hear a rowdy shouting 'To Hell with the Pope', you will be safe in laying a shade of odds that he is not an Orangeman. There is, of course, a jocular toast to which both Catholics and Protestants in the north sometimes give lip service: 'To Hell with the Pope and all the Protestant clergy'. That is regarded as a rather fair and unbiassed expression of sentiment.

While the complications of the case were extensive, the object for which the deputation I have mentioned sought my Lodge's support was the reinstatement of an Orangeman who had been dismissed by the Northern Government. Their case really was based on the contention that, as an Orangeman, the victim should have been more favourably treated. My brethren attacked the deputation with great verbal energy. 'An Orangeman,' they said, 'is not entitled to special treatment; that is not the meaning of civil and religious liberty. The law is superior to any organisation, Orange or otherwise.' If I had not had a high regard for the Orange Order previously, I certainly would have had it since that night.

I think this Lodge of mine walked to the Field but once. Men who were too lazy to carry their banner one year were too

lazy to walk the next. However, I was there many times. As a
boy of twelve or thirteen years I walked to Craigavon, long
since a home for soldiers wounded in the last war, carrying the
string of a banner (secured for me by our milk-man), for which,
to my surprise, I received the noble sum of one shilling. At the
Field, a slightly older boy, a Nationalist on whose kitchen
mantelpiece was pasted a piece of propaganda headed, 'Was the
Battle of the Boyne a Protestant victory?' and in whose parlour
was a picture of Jim Larkin (a terrible offence), offered me half-
a-crown if I would allow him to have my banner-string on the
way home. He had become infected with the spirit of the day!
At Craigavon that day, a really historic 'Twelfth', although
I did not know it at the time, I met a Roman Catholic van-
driver of my acquaintance. He was playing a flute in a band
accompanying one of the Lodges.

I once helped to sell minerals and sandwiches from a roadside stall near the Field, which was being run for some sort of
charity. That meant leaving Belfast at 3 a.m., pushing a hand-
cart full of food and drink, and returning near midnight when
nothing remained of the day's celebrations but the loyal arches
across the streets and a lot of orange peel in the gutters.

On yet another occasion I played a bugle in a Boy Scout
band which accompanied a Lodge. There was a lot of trouble
over that. The Scout Commissioner complained that as the
organisation was non-political and interdenominational Boy
Scouts should have nothing to do with an Orange procession.
He was quite correct. The fuss blew over after we had offered
airy — and hairy — excuses about taking part in the procession
merely for the money which we received for our services.

The annual walk to the Field on the Twelfth of July has
neither the political nor religious significance which those un-
acquainted with the Order seem to imagine. No one listens to
the speeches. It is a holiday celebration, with a lot of exercise
attached to it. It is musical and colourful. The Lambeg drums
are condemned for their barbaric noise by most Orangemen,
and they are used by very few Lodges. Most of the Lodges hire
the services of really excellent bands. The banners, of course,
are a riot of colour, even if some of the illustrations are taken
as a joke nowadays, such as that of Queen Victoria handing a
Bible to a black subject of hers over a scroll proclaiming that
this is 'the secret of England's greatness'. The principal part

of the proceedings at the Field is lunch. My Lodge did it in style, with chicken and ham served by a reputable caterer, a trifle to follow, and a reasonable number of bottles of stout.

My most happy recollection of the Twelfth is of an occasion when myself and another youth — I think his name was 'Francey' Stewart and that he was an apprentice riveter in the Queen's Island — picked up two pleasing wenches at the Field and took them to a lonely lane near Finaghy for a sweet and sweaty piece of love-making. My most unpleasant recollection is of an occasion when, very young, I was allowed to walk in the ranks of a Lodge of which a friend's father was Worshipful Master. One of the members drank too much in the Field and was a source of disturbance to the rest of the Lodge and of terror to me on the long walk home from Holywood.

For a time I was lay chaplain to an Orange Lodge, and I recall a few words of our monthly prayer for the unfortunate Papists: 'Deliver, we pray Thee, the children of the Church of Rome from error and false doctrine.' There may have been something, too, about 'assuage their malice' and 'confound their devices'. But, again, on that point my poor old memory is not clear.

While religion continues to be taken as seriously as it is in this country there is a definite necessity for the Orange Order, if Protestantism is not to disappear completely through mixed marriages, emigration and birth control. So far as individual Roman Catholics are concerned, it is a harmless institution. A friend of mine once met a sailor in a city hotel and brought him out to an Orange dinner. Nearly three hours elapsed before the sailor discovered that he was at a Protestant function, and he then told my friend that he was a Roman Catholic. When the news spread, we drank a toast to him and everyone was happy.

CAMPBELL BARTON made only one contribution to *The Bell*, in May 1943. I have not been able either to trace him or to discover any other work by him under that name. The piece describes the combined folk-art and -practice that in quieter times made the Orangemen's processions a colourful pageant and not an assertion of racial superiority.

AN ARCH PURPLE PAST   Campbell Barton   *May 1943*

THIS HOURE HER VIGILL
By VALENTIN IREMONGER

Elizabeth, frigidly stretched,
On a spring day surprised us
With her starched dignity and the quietness
Of her hands, clasping a black cross.

With a book and candle and holy-water dish
She received us in the room with the blind down.
Her eyes were peculiarly closed and we knelt shyly
Noticing the blot of her hair on the white pillow.

We met that evening by the crumbling wall
In the field behind the house where I lived
And talked it over but could find no reason
Why she had left us whom she had liked so much.

Death, yes, we understood: something to do
With age and decay, decrepit bodies.
But here was this vigorous one, aloof and prim,
Who would not answer our furtive whispers.

Next morning, hearing the priest call her name,
I fled outside being full of certainty
And cried my seven years against the church's stone wall.
For eighteen years I did not speak her name

Until this autumn day, when, in a gale,
A sapling fell outside my window, its branches
Rebelliously blotting the lawn's green. Suddenly, I thought
Of Elizabeth, frigidly stretched.

VALENTIN IREMONGER was born in Sandymount in 1918. After a distinguished theatrical career as writer, actor and director he joined the Irish Foreign Service in 1946 and has served as Irish Ambassador in Scandinavia, India and at present is ambassador to Luxembourg. His poetry appeared mostly in *The Bell* and *The Irish Times* and both it and his critical work were important influences on the post-Yeatsian generation. He translated from the Irish the book *The Hard Road to the Klondike* and *An Irish Navvy*. His latest production is an LP of his poems read by himself entitled *By Sandymount Strand*.

THIS HOURE HER VIGILL   *Valentin Iremonger*   *October 1943*

WORKING CLASS
By JAMES PLUNKETT

A T three o'clock that morning Joey knew his father was dead. For four whole months through the heat of July to the creeping chill of October they had nursed the sick man, his mother and his sister and sometimes himself taking it in turns to watch through the night. He knew it when he awoke to find the darkness around him vibrating with shocked terror, to hear the piteous crying of his sister through the plywood partition which divided his room from theirs. He had dressed himself hurriedly, his throat dry and hard with the dread of death, and had gone into the room. It was heavy with the smell of living, and yellow with lamplight. Already the tenement was astir, doors creaking softly open and floors thudding with the heavy tread of half awakened people. When his mother saw him she began to sob wildly. She clapped her hands as dealers in the streets do when they are quarrelling, while the hair she had loosened streamed about her face.

'Look at your poor father, sweet Jesus have mercy on him! he's gone, he's gone, he's gone.' Her barbaric grief and her screeching shattered his taut nerves. 'O sorra to night me poor boy and your sweet father cold and dead. A sorra this night and him stiff and could in his bed. A sorra sorra sorra sorra....'

He had stood transfixed until her keening died away. Then he went over and put his arms around her and around his sister, feeling the comfort which their forlornness craved stealing and creeping from his body into theirs, their tears hot on his hands and his throat. His mind had ceased to work at the sight of the twisted thing in the bed, and he could not talk to them, but he stroked their heads and petted them and murmured over and over, 'Hush you now, sure hush you, there now, there now.' Gradually in response to the movement of his hands and the instinctive chanting of his voice they grew restful and their breathing softened and became tranquil. Then Mrs. Nolan shuffled in, smelling of age and snuff, her yellow face with its wrinkles seamed with dirt framed in the black shawl she had draped over her head. In one movement she cast the shawl from her and threw out her hands to form an abandoned cross. She held the attitude for a moment while she murmured sympathy. She crossed the room and took charge of affairs. This was her regular occupation since her own husband had died over twenty years ago.

Now it was evening. His father was stretched and habited, with rosary beads entwined in his joined hands. − Now it was evening and the atmosphere of death was on the room. Joey sat very straight and quiet in his favourite corner, his small body thin and childish despite his thirty years, his neatly kept suit threadbare and greasy in the lamplight, his face hard and set but betraying no emotion. The room was full of people, yet no one noticed him. When they came in they said:

'I'm sorry for your trouble, Mrs. Byrne. And sure, poor Mary, it's you'll miss your father,' and then as an afterthought they might say, 'And Joey.' Then they talked to Mary or one of the neighbours and pretended surprise when the glass was thrust into their hands.

The air was heavy with the smell of tobacco and with the sour-sweet odour of candle and corpse. His mother sat by the bedside, her eyes fixed on the years that had passed. Her fat fingers swayed slightly from side to side in rhythm with the murmurings of her endless rosaries, her beads slipping mechanically through fingers reddened and coarse from work. Mary was all business, very superior in black mourning dress,

treating the neighbours she tended with aloofness, except Tom
Keegan, who was secretary of his father's Union. Already she
seemed more independent, more the young lady of the house,
because only her father could, with one gesture, have put her
in her place, jeer the harm out of her highflying notions.

They were all talking and laughing as they drank, only his
mother remained detached. Something in her detachment told
Joey, but as yet he was unable to resolve the thought. Ted
Byrne, whom his father had saved from unemployment many
times, was urging his butty Foley to sing. Toucher Flynn, with
a bowler pushed back on his head, his face all bulbous nose and
sweat, his full moustache glistening and his corduroy trousers
spotted with the beer he was mouthing, coming now and then
to nudge and whisper to Bridie McGovern, Bridie that would
never have got her full Widow's Pension if it were not for his
father. They all owed something to his father. They all came to
his father in their trouble. Because he was once a Union official
they thought they had the right to worry him with every foot-
ling little difficulty they were too lazy to solve for themselves.
But now it was evening and his father was gone, and not one of
them cared a tinker's damn. They were drunk and wanted fun.
Toucher gurgled in his throat and slapped Rat Foley on the
back.

'Gwan,' he shouted, 'Gwan to hell Rat. Sing.' He indicated
the dead man with his thumb. 'There's the man that could make
Rat sing.' He raised his hat solemnly. 'Couldn't he Rat? —
Bejakus Rat, but yeh sung fine and hard when he hauled yeh
out of Dowling's in 1913. Yeh sung fine and hard then, my
boyo!' The room guffawed thinking how the dead man had
beaten up Rat until he howled that night for whining about the
starvation caused by the strike. Rat's little eyes glittered a
second with malice. Then he was tentative. 'Well, now, Mr.
Flynn, if yeh reely want, if the present company...'

'The boul' man Rat.'

'A few bars...'

'Ninety-Eight, Rat.'

'In everlastin' honour iv the dead...'

'Aisy now, aisy, give the man a hearin'.'

A shuffling of shairs, spitting, sniffling, coughing, the
murmur dying and Rat's voice breaking on the muteness of
smoke and smell and heat.

"Who fears to speak iv ninety-eight
    Who blushes at the name."

His eyes shining, his thin white face oozing and tilted up-
ward, his tiny mouth agape, a shudder of emotion creeping
through the room.

"But *threw* men like *yew* men..."

Toucher had crossed the room and was leaning over Joey.
He was tapping him on the shoulder.
    'Aw Joey son, but it's you'll miss yer father. Yer father was
a man Joey, a patriot, that's what yer father was. Never was the
likes of him before.' His breath was sour on Joey's face. 'Me
pal, Joey, that's what yer father was, me best pal. Big and wild
and fond of his sup − ach, doesn't matter a curse, Joey − a
darlin' fighter, Joey, that's what he was, with a big heart for
the poor and the misfortunate. There was a father to be proud
of, Joey son, there was a pal for yeh.' His mouth was a yawn of
yellow molars. "Dan," he'd say to me, "yer a faithful oul
sowdger Dan, that stood by me to the bitther end in the
troubles of thirteen, an yeh'd folly me to the grave." And I
would, Joey, I would. Aye and beyont, Joey. That's poor Dan
Flynn for yeh.'
    The song faded from the room and it quickened with
applause. It was a Bedlam of smells, smoke haze, sour candle,
greasy faces. Mary and Tom Keegan whispering. His mother
unmoving and strangely unmoved. Her liking for her husband
shuddered on their marriage bed and broke in the bitterness
of wild drinking bouts and labour quarrels. Joey had never
thought that before but now he knew. There was another
thought troubling him too, but what it was escaped him. It
concerned his father. He tried to resolve it. He stared hard at
the memory of his father. Still the thought eluded him. Toucher
had reeled across the room, was wiping a tear from his face,
was swaying back and forward and speaking to the corpse.
    'Michael oul son, is this what it's come to? Is this how it is
with yeh, chum iv me youth? Bosum pals we was Michael, me
oul sagusher, bosum pals.' The voice reeled off into tipsy song.
'Cumrades, cum-rades, ever since we was... Come on to hell,
Rat. Sing. Give us another.' His eyes were bloodshot. They

glared at the gathering. 'Come on, a hand for Rat, a little encouragement for Rat.' He grinned broadly at nothing. His mouth fell open. 'Bejakus,' he said, and went back to Joey. Rat was singing again...

Later, when they were coming back from the chapel Toucher said, 'That's the beginnin' of a long journey for your Da, Joey. Begod, it's the first time in twenty years he was in the chapel, and then yiz had to carry him there. Begod!' Joey was frozen and silent. He had watched them when the coffin arrived, the shamed way they crept from the room when his father was being moved from bed to coffin. He had heard the scream of his mother when the first dull tap drove the first screw home, but she did not scream for his father, it was for the mere horror of death. Because he loved his father and saw suddenly the emptiness which was coming, his own heart had kicked and something sliced his throat. He heard the rest following when they carried it downstairs, and heard Toucher with drunken devilment saying, 'Bejakus, Michael, I seen yeh canned before, but never boxed.' Some of them tittered at that, but not openly. It was the titter of their daughters in a picture house when the word 'baby' is mentioned. In the chapel again they snivelled and were sad and prayed for the soul which they secretly considered damned, and after that they dispersed and later on they would trickle back to drink and sing and be merry.

Meanwhile Toucher was growing impatient with Joey's silence.

'Aw, Joey, but yer terrible silent. Yeh'd think yeh didn't care a dam' about yer poor Da. Lookit — we'll have a drink to cheer us up, how's that?'

'No,' said Joey. His voice was tired. 'No, Dan.'

'Aw, Joey. Yer a queer chisler. Not like yer father. Haven't his guts, no, nor his feelin' for the worker.'

'Me father was a fool to bother his behind about the whole lousy lot of them!'

'Aw, Joey, yer upset, yeh wouldn't talk like that...'

Joey shrugged. His father had toiled his life away for them and they drove him to hell for it. His father was a great man who wasted greatness on them. His father had brains and their cunning had stolen and exploited them. They used him and then ratted on him. Toucher's eyes were suddenly glimmering with cunning.

'Joey, son.' he said. 'I didn't remark it before, but yer father owed me somethin' well — not much, just a little — well —'

'How much?'

'Aw, well, Joey.' Toucher eyed him uncertainly, his hands moving vaguely. 'It was three bob, Joey. Jus' a little debt...'

Joey had five shillings in his pocket, two two shilling pieces and a single shilling. He took the money out and gave Toucher the shilling and a two shilling piece. He said nothing. Toucher was mealymouthed.

'Aw thanks, Joey, oul' son. I'm not the one to talk about things like that, but times is hard an' well yeh know how it is, Joey.'

Disgust suddenly choking him, Joey swung away.

'For Christ's sake go away, Toucher!' he said. 'You make me sick.'

He rushed out. He stopped when he reached the wall which flanked the river and leaned his elbows on it, watching the flickering of fine rain on the dark limbo of waters. He began to remember things. Little pictures of his youth, scraps of conversation, odds and ends that were almost forgotten. He remembered how his father had tried to teach him to follow in his footsteps and how in the end he had said sadly, wearily:

'All right, son, you don't mind about Trade Unionism and the working class and the bloody freedom of small nations. You just stick to your plastering and your commonsense. You're not cut out for this agitation business, and maybe it's just as well. Sometimes I'm not sure that they're worth it.'

His father had said that and now his father was dead...

A drunken woman with a shawl was approaching him. She brushed against him, stared at him foolishly for a moment, muttered and went on. When she had gone he buried his face in his hands. He was crying, but not for his father alone. He was crying for the emptiness his father had left, for a drunken woman, for himself, and for a whole lost people.

JAMES PLUNKETT (born J. P. Kelly in 1920) hails from Dublin and has been in his time a professional viola player, a trade union official and a producer for RTE. His earlier literary fame was based upon a number of powerful short stories, most of them (thirteen in all) written for *The Bell* between 1942 and 1954. The issue of October 1954 was given over entirely to five of his stories, led by the near novella, 'The Eagle and the Trumpets'. These were later published in two collections, the first called by the story just named, the second after another *Bell* story *The Trusting and the Maimed* (1959). He has shown a continuing interest in the career and character of Jim Larkin, the great Labour organiser of pre-war Dublin, and his involvement in the great lock-out of 1913. *The Risen People* (1958) based upon Larkin's active period in Ireland is still popular. *Strumpet City,* his first novel, and set in the same time, was written in 1969 and got much deserved publicity. *Farewell Companions* (1977) is another Dublin novel set between the wars. In 1978 his *Collected Short Stories* were published. 'Working Class' is very much 'an apprentice piece, though there are acceptable parts of it'. In spite of extreme reluctance Plunkett agreed to its publication because it was typical of the beginnings that many young writers made in *The Bell.* He lives in Kilmacanogue, Co. Wicklow.

WORKING CLASS   James Plunkett   October 1943

THE OPEN WINDOW
By MICHAEL FARRELL ('GULLIVER')

'This is Liberty Hall, gentlemen; you may do as you please here.'
— *She Stoops to Conquer.*

THAT man has a mind like a sewing-machine, said W. B. Yeats, of a famous living English writer whom I will not name. My own mind, less efficient than a machine, is just now like a sewing-bag, and this because of a cat. A friend was chatting one night about the Exhibition of French pictures which is being held in the National College of Art this month. Having told me that pictures by the French Impressionists (who are scarcely 'modern'), would form a large part of the exhibition, he then said that the display would include a water-colour study which Manet made for the famous 'Olympia' painting in the Louvre. I was astonished to hear that there existed a water-colour study of 'Olympia'. It should be most interesting to see. At once I thought of the cat which stands on the end of the couch where the nude, unvoluptuous little courtesan reclines. The glittering eyes staring out at you, the arched black back, and the black tail in a question mark rising beside the indescribable colour of the dress worn by the negress servant. Unforgettable and bewildering cat.

Far be it from me to be that sort of commentator who ascribes to the creations of artists themes which the artists never knew. (Remember Hazlitt? *If we wish to see the force of human greatness we may read Shakespeare; if we wish to see the folly of human learning we may study his commentators.)* But I confess that I have often wondered if 'Olympia's' arched black cat may not possibly be the one comment in this picture devoid of comment, devoid of emotion, a masterpiece of outward fact, marvellously painted. What a fuss they made about it in the 1860's when that sallow schemer, Napoleon's nephew, was letting Baron Haussmann (yes, the Boulevard is in his name) create modern Paris, and providing in his gaslit, waltzing, slightly raffish Empire, one of those attributes of the Stage Frenchman which still linger on the stage — the pointed beard and moustache (together making an upright pick-axe), *the Imperial.*

BEFORE *Olympia* there had come Manet's famous picnic-scene, the 'Dejeuner sur l'herbe' which also caused enormous ado because 'the men are dressed but the woman is naked.' When artists immediately pointed to Giorgione's famous 'Fete Champetre' (English people sometimes call it 'The Open-air Concert'), the objectors said, 'Ah, but Giorgione's men are in Fancy-dress.' This uproariously funny argument, equating female nudity to male Fancy-Dress, completely overlooked the fact that Giorgione's men were wearing the dress of Giorgione's period!

Lord, how much these unco' guid objectors resemble one another in all generations, and, dear hearts, how funny they are. I remember a certain Dublin 'Catholic' paper at the time of the R.D.S. bi-centenary celebrations at Ballsbridge, just at the time when women had the temporary fashion of beach pyjamas. *While Scoutmasters and Freemasons hold licentious orgies at Ballsbridge there are women ready to desecrate our littoral by walking there in the bi-furcated garments of lubricity.'* The

writer of that should be subsidised by the State for adding to the store of public hilarity.

However, some people claim that here and there we show signs of recovering lost ground. Brieux' 'Damaged Goods' has been banned here as a book: but a few weeks later it was produced, without interference, as a play. That is a welcome snub to our literary Censors, and shows that there is still some common-sense in Ireland.

THAT damned cat is back again, fussing and mussing in my sewing-bag mind. It sets me to ask you if there are for you certain pictures which, when seen in memory, seem to be 'stolen' by some detail which was not the main object of the painter's eye? To illustrate, let me keep to animals in our promised exhibition. Gauguin's 'White Hose' being the main object, obviously won't do, nor Degas' horses in meadows or under carriages, though I hope our exhibition will have some examples of his race-course period and not be all ballet, much as I like his unforgettable 'Lessons', his 'back-stages', and that long perspectival dancing-lesson picture in the Louvre. (It's up in those three marvellous rooms where the Camondo Collection of the 19th Century reigns, one storey above the kingdom of Poussin and Claude Lorrain.) Again, one could not mark scores for Leonardo's horses, etc., but I do count the marvellous beastie, that sleek and predatory, that stoatish, ancient and Ermine beast, which Cecilia Galleriani holds in her arms in Leonardo's portrait of her. I have seen the picture only in reproductions. The original is in Cracow, or was up to 1939. Cecilia was one famous mistress of that dark Ludovico whom Milan called 'The Moor'. Again in Dore's famous illustrations for Don Quixote, I shouldn't count Quixote's horse Rosinante or Sancho's ass, but the roosting hens which Dore put into the inn-yard at night. As for the French Impressionists in our promised exhibition – well, we will have a copy of Manet's 'Woman with the Parrot'? And the woman in black with the two great white dogs? Has Manet animals in other pictures? What of Monet, he who could paint all that deep distance around the 'Bridge at Argenteuil' without as much as a dog's tail showing? (Think of the dog Gainsborough or Constable would have shown.) Renoir could paint the woman and child of the terrace with the trees and river beyond, and not put one bird or branch or water. In Sisley's snow-effects, not a hungry robin; not a dog nor a horse along his canals; not a cow in the fields; under his bridges no fish. (Could Turner have painted a brook without an animal somewhere?) In fact, did the Impressionists, excluding Manet and Degas, ever see an animal? (Courbet, their predecessor, said: *Angels? But I've never seen angels. So I can't paint them.*)

COMING thus upon Courbet in the sewing-bag has revived in me an old curiosity about the woman who was for him the 'Femme d'Irlande'. I speak of 'Joe', the mistress of his friend Whistler. Joanna, Mrs. Abbot, the 'Joe' who was *Irish, Roman Catholic, the daughter of a sort of Captain Costigan*. What sort of 'a sort of Captain Costigan' did E. R. and J. Pennell mean in their official Life of Whistler (Heinemann, 1808)? Surely not an advance-guard of the army of O'Casey's Captain Boyle? Over and over again Whistler painted 'Joe', nearly as often as Rembrandt painted Saskia. In the famous 'Wapping', which only Americans of Baltimore can now see in the original, 'Joe', with her copper-coloured hair and the *strange beauty* which Whistler tried to describe to Fantin-Latour, leans back from the table on the overhanging balcony of the Angel Inn, below her the Thames shipping, beside her the two men, one of whom was Legros himself. That copper-coloured hair and *strange beauty* caught Courbet who painted her as 'Jo, Femme d'Irlande' (she became 'the Irish type'

to him) and again as 'La Belle Irlandaise'. She was Whistler's famous 'White Girl' and also the even more famous 'The Little White Girl'. Described as – *A woman of next to no education but of keen intelligence, which separated her from the Irish narrowness, with great charm of manner and so well-read that before she met Whistler she knew more about painting than many of its professed connoisseurs.* But what really tickles my curiosity is, '*daughter of a sort of Captain Costigan*'. Who will lighten my dark ignorance, please?

I DON'T know why my sewing-bag mind has leaped to Lausanne. But I am suddenly thinking how, in the last war, the towns of Switzerland, especially Lausanne and Geneva, experienced an unaccustomed, and fevered, stylishness because, thanks to Switzerland's geographical position, its cities became centres for journalists, diplomatists and their wives (or 'nieces'), spies, counter-spies, escapers, intriguers, wealthy internees, 'peace-feeling' messengers and so on. I am told that this was has not caused anywhere quite so much 'atmosphere', but that what there is, is mainly to be found in Stockholm. The temporary disappearance of Europe's traditional frontiers after 1940 reduced the importance of Switzerland. Diplomacy, spying, journalism and adventure move now on the perimeter of Europe, not in the centre, and Stockholm, encircled by belligerents, has taken the place held by Switzerland last time. Consider only journalism. Before the war, Stockholm had a small, though very active and well-informed, number of native journalists and very few foreign Pressmen. To-day the foreign journalists alone number 500. Each of the big agencies has several men there and in addition to representatives of the major belligerents, there are journalists sent from London by the exile papers of Norway, Denmark, Holland and Belgium. The Foreign Office provides an excellently-equipped Press room at the Grand Hotel, and there the representatives of 'opposite sides' work under an unwritten law of 'non-interference'. In addition to the geographical situation Sweden has another attraction – the freedom of its Press which gives not only full reports from its own and other journalists in every country of the world but also expresses opinions freely.

THE remark of Yeats which I quoted as I began was, I think, very unfair. He was often excessively unfair. James Agate has been quoting the Yeatsian verdict on the Hamlet of the late Sir John Martin-Harvey: *like a rabbit with a thunderbolt tied to its tail.* A truer, as well as kinder, description would have been *like a wren hurrying from the wren-boys.* I think W. B. Yeats was often wilfully resistant to the elemental appeal of *the theatre.* I thought that Harvey's Hamlet was theatrically effective and that behind the Edwardian technique there was much understanding and poetical feeling. And there was this about his performance, as compared with some – it had a feeling for nobility. His Hamlet I thought wistful and frail, despite the physical frame-work. The Cambridge undergraduates of the A.D.C. theatre were indignant with me when I, meaning only honest flattery, said that their Hamlet bore a remarkable resemblance to Harvey's. Aren't we all a little unfair to Harvey just because of *The Only Way?* I suppose you know that it was he himself who made that now famous adaptation of Dickens' *A Tale of Two Cities.* Dublin loved it, and loved him in *The Corsican Brothers,* in *After All* and in *A Cigarette-Maker's Romance,* which were done at the old Theatre Royal. His last performance here was at the Gaiety in the year before the war, when he gave his famous rendering of the Burgomaster in Maeterlinck's *The Burgomaster of Stilemonde.* It's not uninteresting to note that the year when the Burgomaster first appeared at La Scala, London, was the year when Harvey's beloved teacher, Irving, died

– 1919. And now up from the sewing-bag comes an inquiry. In that A.D.C. Theatre in Cambridge the women's parts are played by youths and young men as they were between about 600 A.D. and the 17th Century. (The custom lingered on in places through the 18th and spurted again in the 19th Centuries!) Does any reader know whether other theatres in Europe or America have this custom to-day?

A CORRESPONDENT kindly answers one of the questions which I put last month on behalf of some readers: *The word 'teetotal' did not come from a stammerer trying to say 'total'. It began 100 years ago. A Mr. Turner was advocating Total Abstinence. He wished to be emphatic and he deliberately said 'tee-tee-tee-total abstinence'. A little later, Queen Victoria received a deputation of Abstainers and the 'London Times' reported it as 'a deputation of teetotal abstainers'. From then on, the word became ordinary English.* Thanks very much. Will my Tipperary reader please note this interesting answer to his question?

THAT cat is back again; pussing around the sewing-bag; Olympia's cat; Gulliver's cat. (Do go to the exhibition and look at that damned cat.) This time it brings out George Moore, Normandy and, alas, war. To be precise, Rouen. That town which now I bid you name 'A little Ireland in France'. Not far from St. Patrick's church where the stained-glass windows (not often good in France, but good here), show St. Patrick baptising Oengus (yes, the pastoral staff pierces the Irish Prince's foot), St. Patrick being carried off to Ireland, herding the swine, being offered the poisoned cup by Laoghaire's attendant, and so on – not far from that is the Gallery beside the Park where George Moore, in Blanche's portrait of him, looks, in his own words, *like a drunken cabby.* Rouen of St. Laurence O'Toole's exile and death. (His ashes are in a shrine in his church St. Laurent, in Eu, close-by.) Rouen cruelly savaged, raped, etc., by the Irish soldiers of the Butlers, while, just as at home, a Desmond was on the other side within the besieged city. That was the famous Thomas, 5th Earl, who loved and married Catherine Cormack, a cottager's daughter, an 'offence' for which the Irish revolted against him.

> *By the Feale's wave benighted*
> *No star in the skies*
> *To thy door by love lighted*
> *I first saw thy eyes.*

Yes, the man of Tom Moore's song. Rouen to which the Flying Earls came by boat up from the mouth of the Seine where armies boat and match to-day. Rouen of the Irish bishops, Irish manu-scripts, of General Kilmaine and that gallant, unfortunate Lally of Tuam. And Tone! Dining and planning there with Lord Edward. Name upon Irish name rising out of the mass of our lost, aban-doned past to tease the heart with regrets for what we might have become. Links with the dim shape of an Irish 'foreign policy'. And between Rouen and charming Caen, all those orchards, those fields where I sat on the hay-stacks drinking cider and winking down at the sturdy farm-girls while all

the bells of Caen sent the Angelus through the sunset.

> *Ave Maria! Over earth and sea,*
> *That heavenliest hour of heaven*
> *Is worthiest thee*

Millet's painting of the Angelus by sunset in the French fields is sentimental in execution but not in reality, any more than is the as yet unpictured reality when an Irishman bares his head in fields by the Nore as the bell sounds from ancient Kilkenny.

Can there be heard now in Normandy above the sounds of war the call to that lovely prayer? It will be heard again in peace. But will it happen ever again that a wandering Irishman, tired from a long day on Italian roads, may come to a little hilly town by evening, find that its name is Pistoia and, entering the church, suddenly see there the Blessed Virgin forever receiving the tidings of the Annunciation, forever carved by the genius of Della Robbia? Bells and stone, speaking the spirit of religion, carrying heart and mind far from those tongues and pens which, while invoking the name of Christianity... But let us leave the window wide open on that happy Italian sky. Like those lovely last lines of *Uncle Vanya* we, too, sometime if not in our time will have rest, will have rest...

MICHAEL FARRELL was born in 1900 and is best known to the present generation as the author of *Thy Tears might Cease* (1963) the mammoth Irish novel that was quarried out of an even greater pile of manuscript by Monk Gibbon. He was for many years a contributor to *The Bell,* first as a kind of amateur drama correspondent and later as 'Gulliver' the presenter of the feature *The Open Window* which began in January 1943 and ran regularly till 1954. It was a free-ranging literary causerie which took as its motto Mr. Hardcastle's offer to the young gallants, Marlowe and Hastings, who took his house for an inn in *She Stoops to Conquer,* 'This is Liberty Hall, gentlemen: you may do as you please here!' It and its founder lived up to its title. Farrell died in 1962.

I DID PENAL SERVITUDE

By 'D83222'

G ET up in the van, you blighters.' The warder turned to
me. 'Come on, Ronan, you fat sow. Climb up. You'll
have to move quicker when you get to the Bog.'

'The Bog?' I asked.

'The Bog is Portlaoighise Prison,' he rplied. 'Mountjoy "The
Joy," Dundrum "The Drum," Grangegorman "The Gorman".'

We scrambled into the prison van and started for Kingsbridge.
'Thank goodness we're finished with Mountjoy,' I murmured.
The warder turned on me like a mother defending her young.

'The Joy's all right,' he said angrily. 'Wait till you get to the
Bog. There's where you'll know what discipline means. You'll
get "The Digger" and a kick in the backside if you sneeze
sideways. You'll have to be on your toes there all the time.'
He chuckled and grew expansive. 'When you get to the Bog
you'll be brought before "Big———" (The Governor). I'll tell
you word for word the little piece he'll recite to you.' He here
gave me, as I later found, a perfect imitation of the Governor's
accent. ' "You have not been in trouble before. You have been
transferred to us from a local prison. You will find life here
somewhat different. For one thing the discipline is much
stricter. But if it is I think you will find the living conditions
much better. If you want to know anything consult a warder,
a principal, the Chief or myself. Do not ask advice from other
convicts. The old lags will give you wrong advice and then
laugh when you find yourself in trouble. If you keep the rules
the time will pass quickly enough. If you break the rules I can
assure you, my friends, that we will make you very sorry for
yourselves, indeed. Take them away." '

As he finished, the prison van arrived at Kingsbridge. Being a special select first offender, I was handcuffed alone. The other two prisoners were also first offenders, but their offences did not come under the heading of 'clean crimes' like mine so they were in a lower class and would not be permitted to associate with me. They were handcuffed together, and as one man was very fat and the other very small they had extreme difficulty in getting down from the van. Like two spanceled goats dragging against one another over a fence, these poor fellows winced with pain as they struggled down. We were put standing in front of the booking office while the warder arranged about tickets or passes. We had a detective and some Civic Guards with us. In our dreadful prison frieze and horrible caps we were a conspicuous sight. Every person coming to the booking office stared at us. The fat prisoner was well known on the Limerick line. Several people recognised him and nudged their companions to have a look. At last we got on the platform.

Then our ordeal and agony really commenced. The warder seemed to think there was a special carriage engaged for us. The Mallow Races were on that day. The train was crowded. The warder walked us slowly up and down the full length of that long train but he still failed to find the reserved carriage. Every head was out of the carriage and corridor windows to stare at the peep show. You know that poem *Maud Muller* by the American poet Whittier containing the lines:-

> *'Of all the sad words of tongue or pen; the saddest are*
> *these,*
> *It might have been.'*

I had learnt it from beginning to end the previous evening in Mountjoy. I now repeated it slowly word by word to keep myself sane. The fat prisoner who had been a man of position before his lapse kept repeating, 'Christ Jesus have mercy on us. Christ Jesus have mercy on us.'

The Civic Guards and detectives who accompanied us were decent men with human feelings. They turned angrily on the warder.

'For God's sake do something, and stop making an exhibition of these poor devils before the whole train.'

The warder pushed us into a fairly empty corridor-carriage. People crowded around us. A tall thin dyspeptic-looking crank

of a man demanded angrily that we be removed. 'I am keeping
these seats for friends who will be back in a moment.' A lady
held up a little child to see what the row was about.

'Who are the funny men, Mammy?' lisped the child.

'Hush, darling,' came in a stage whisper from the soothing
mother, 'I think they are lunatics!'

The warder hustled us out again. Up and down the platform
again, up and down. At last a railway official found a carriage.
Some bookmakers and their clerks made room for us. The
corridor was crowded and as the fat prisoner's case had created
a stir in the press a constant stream of passengers pretended to
look for the toilet and stopped outside our carriage to peep in
at us. Men do not change in appearance when they are found
out. You could see the disappointment registering on the faces
of the morbid crowd when they realised that we had not
grown horns on our foreheads or cloven feet. One of the
bookies, who looked as if he lifted his elbow too often,
produced cigarettes and offered them to us. Two of us were
non-smokers but the undersized prisoner grasped eagerly at the
last 'fag' he would smoke for two years and three months. The
warder commenced an argument about Eire's Constitution with
a bookie's clerk.

The clerk was inclined to be communistic. The warder held
that Eire was the most Christian country in the world and that
our Christian Constitution was an example to the rest of
mankind. I thought of that parade up and down the platform
and of the little innocent child's amazement at our dreadful
degrading clothes. I thought of Our Lord and Mary Magdalen
and wondered what He must think of the things done in His
name.

A man I knew in my heyday came into the carriage to speak
to the friendly bookie. The latter produced a flat bottle of
whiskey from his hip pocket and offered my former friend a
drink. My friend declined with thanks stating emphatically
that he had given up drink and was definitely 'on the water-
waggon' for life. Then suddenly he saw me. He took a moment
or two to realise that this man in shame's uniform was the same
Ronan who had 'seen his full house' in the Grand in Tramore
last 15th of August. Then he swore 'pledge be damned' took
the bottle of whiskey from the bookmaker, drained it at one
swig, and by the time we got to Portlaoighise, he was a very

drunk man indeed.

From the time we left Kingsbridge until we reached our destination that warder never stopped talking. His monotone haunts me to this day. The bookie looked at his watch and swore that if the train would not hurry up he would miss the first race. I reflected on the time, so short ago, when every moment seemed important to me too. And now time was of no consequence at all. In prison we got an hour and a half for meals that took five minutes to eat. We were brought to the chapel half an hour before Mass. If we complained of the slightest ailment we were locked up as 'Sick in Cell' until the doctor saw us hours afterwards. When we became inmates of Portlaoighise prison we would be locked up every Sunday, Church Holyday and Bank Holiday from 12.30 in the afternoon until 7 o'clock next morning. On my very first day in prison I realised how little time really matters. At three o'clock on a glorious summer afternoon my clothes were taken from me. I was given only a short shirt to wear. There was nothing to do but to get into bed. As I lay there I wondered if the busy hurrying world was all wrong and if these prison institutions were on the right track with their Yogi contempt for time.

At last we arrived at Portlaoighise.

'Goodbye, you poor bastards,' said the genial bookmaker. The warder looked wonderingly at him. Then it dawned slowly on him that this bookie had sympathy for us. For thirty years prisoners were just numbers to that warder. 'One on' when a man came. 'One off' when a man died or was released. The men who passed through prisons had long since ceased to appear human beings in his eyes. He looked on them impersonally, not as real people: as a Bank Official going on the 'Exchanges' secures his own thirty shillings in an inside pocket with a safety pin, while at the same time he carries a thousand pounds of the Bank's money carelessly in his outside pocket. At the same time that warder is a decent man to his wife, family and neighbours. He struggled for a moment to see the bookie's point of view. But thirty years of routine and red tape won the battle in his dull brain.

'Come on, you bastards,' he ordered. 'On the double.'

We got out of the train. Some Portlaoighise prison warders awaited us. More were hanging around the platform. Then we were marched ahead of our keepers through the town a full quarter of a mile to the prison. It seemed to me that every small boy in the County Leix arrived for the occasion. Small boys are primitive, realistic, callous and cruel. They danced around us and pointed and jeered. Little dirty-nosed girls dragged smaller snivelling infants forward to witness the new kind of circus and peepshow provided free, gratis and for nothing by the Department of Justice. Behind I could hear the Mountjoy warder recounting to his Portlaoighise confreres how he had proved to a communistic bookie's clerk that ours was a most Christian country. Ahead the fat prisoner was still praying aloud, 'Christ Jesus have mercy on us.' At a graveyard we were about to take a wrong turning. A stout old Portlaoighise warder, with the suns of India on his face, let forth a barrack-square roar at us which must have shook the dead in their graves.

'To the right, you ——————— —————'s.'

At last we were at the massive prison gates. The stout old warder addressed us:—

'Remember, when you go before the Governor say "Sir" — "Sir" all the time and remember you are not in the "Joy" here. "It's "on your toes and on the double" here all the time but you'll have decent, clean food and no lice in your blankets.'

From inside the prison gates there was much peeping through spyholes, shuffling of keys and drawing back of heavy bolts. At last we were admitted. The warder inside looked at us impersonally.

'That will be three on,' he remarked, making an entry in his note-book. The stout warder, in tones that must have struck terror in countless tommies' hearts, roared, 'Quick march. On the double.'

My left boot was hurting me like hell. We shuffled forward. The first stage of my journey to Fear had ended.

IN THE 'BOG'

As I ambled forward I was struck by the beauty of the flowers: for inside the front entrance in Portlaoighise prison there is a lovely flower garden, and this was the month of August. Over the passage-way to the Governor's office there was a canopy of roses. Surely the Bridge of Sighs in Venice

has its counterpart here: with a brilliant sun in the sky this
Bower of Roses should be a trysting place for two Arcadian
lovers not the portal to men's fears and remorse. I promised
myself that if I lived through my sentence I would on the day
I was leaving look back and try to appreciate the beauty of that
arbour. As the front gate opens to let me through, I will turn
back and gaze ion that shaded walk. It will be a cold and wintry
day but in its barren bareness that scene will be more beautiful
in my eyes than in all its summer glory. Roses are for loves'
dreams not convicts' nightmares.

Before we reached the Governor's office we were instructed
by a principal warder. He again impressed on us to say 'Sir'
to the Governor. I already sensed the subtle difference between
Portlaoighise and Mountjoy prisons. Here there was discipline
in the very air. You drank it in. From the outside the very
look of the place is like a Foreign Legion fortress in Morocco.
One of the other prisoners remembering the more humane
ways of Mountjoy tried to make conversation by remarking
on the glorious weather. The warders had not to reprimand
him. They just gave him their 'You're not in the "Joy" now'
look and speech froze on his lips. 'Remember you're not in
Mountjoy here' is a warning that never for one moment is
discipline relaxed in Portlaoighise; but it also expresses a
boastful pride in spotless cleanliness, the best prison food in
Eire and clean-minded, well-behaved educated prisoners to mix
with, instead of the petty snatch-thieves and sewer-rats of
the 'Joy'.

We were marched to the Governor's office. We stood to
attention while a clerk handed him files relative to our cases.
The Governor is a tall thin man with iron grey hair and the
straight cut of an army officer. He never raised his eyes to look
at us, but word for word repeated the little speech the Mountjoy warder had forecast in the Black Maria. 'Beware of the old
lags... If you break the rules, I assure you, my friends, we will
make you very sorry for yourselves indeed... Take them away.'

We were next marched to the prison proper – the old wings
built about one hundred years ago are now used as store-
rooms – the new 'E' block of the prison was built in 1900
and strikes you by its massiveness. Before the main door was
opened we were scrutinised through a peephole which reminded
me of the open-sesame methods of a film speak-easy. Inside

the prisoners were all locked up for dinner. The warders had not yet gone to theirs: there were about thirty of them in uniform but in my eyes they seemed hundreds. A group of them surrounded us and rushed us into our separate cells. An old warder, obviously a one-time Sergeant or Corporal roared at us 'Come on you, take off those lousy Mountjoy rags, and put on the kit there in your cells. Hurry up! I want to get my dinner.'

As we took off our clothes they were carefully searched by two warders. In Mountjoy the prison clothes are often old, torn, and ill-fitting. In Portlaoighise every convict gets a fitted suit of heavy grey frieze, with a thick black stripe. As I was a star select first offender I got in addition a suit of lighter frieze with a narrow black stripe for Sunday and recreation wear. I also got two shirts and two towels with my number stamped upon them. In Mountjoy, however, you get a neat tie. In Portlaoighise I was given a large neckcloth which I had the greatest difficulty in making up like an ordinary tie. I scrambled into my clothes as fast as I could but not quick enough for the 'Charles Laughton' warder at the door. His bull neck grew redder and his blood pressure mounted as he roared 'Come on. For God's sake get a move on!' He forgot me, however, in his horror over the mess the tall young prisoner next door had made of his neckcloth. Instead of making it up like an ordinary tie, this unfortunate had produced a cravat that out-Brummelled Beau Brummell.

In the English-speaking armies there are three words, all unprintable, which form the basic English of the non-commissioned ranks. In prison where so many ex-soldiers are prisoners or warders these three words become monotonous by their constant repetition. There is a story told in Portlaoighise of a young priest who heard a prisoner use an unprintable word. He reprimanded the warder in charge for allowing such obscene language. The warder proceeded to appease the clergyman by saying, 'Ah, don't be too hard on the poor ――― Father; sure that ――― knows no ―――― better.'

Eventually we satisfied our sartorial expert, we were handed our dinners and locked up for about an hour. At two o'clock we were let out to empty our slops at lightning speed and I got a chance of viewing the prison.

There are four storeys: E1, the ground floor, for sexual

offenders, E2 directly above it − the even numbered cells on
E2 for star select first offenders, the odd numbers for old
offenders: the third landing, E3, and fourth landing, E4, are for
local prisoners − that is men not doing penal servitude. On each
landing there is a warder in charge known as a 'Class Officer'.
The E1 class officer now roared 'Odd numbers E1 one pace
forward march!' Like well-trained soldiers twenty-six prisoners
stepped smartly forward. Then the word of command came −
'By the left, quick march!' And the convicts marched to their
different work groups.

My real punishment had begun.

'D83222' was the anonymous author of the true prison experiences
suffered by himself when he was sentenced to three years penal servitude
for embezzlement. The pieces printed in *The Bell* were part of a book
which was printed in 1945 and reprinted in 1946 to great popular and
critical acclaim. Sean O'Faolain allowed the author to use his Dublin
telephone number at the time, 83222, instead of the real number which
might have caused a breach of anonymity; he also wrote a preface for the
book. With Peadar O'Donnell's encouragement, 'D83222' later wrote a
further series of pieces with the general title of 'There But for the Grace
of God' on how he came to qualify for penal servitude. These as carefully
and beautifully written as the book were typical *Bell* exercises ideally
combining excellence with much social relevance. 'D83222 became a
journalist on his release and now lives in Ealing, in West London.

I DID PENAL SERVITUDE 2
'Journey to Fear.   'D83222'   *November 1944*

IN THIS THEIR SEASON
By ROY McFADDEN

Like wind-twirled butterflies the leaves
Swirl and ebb to the ground – Blue smoke
Stands against the sky, a leaf
Bedded with moss-like clouds. Cold sheaves
Of sun fold up and die.

This is the season of an evening's grief
When the whole countryside bends a grave head
In meditation: when the smoking leaf,
The leaves swirling to soil, seem particles
Of the insidious sadness of the dead.

Withering leaves, the grey hills wilt;
And, sidling near them, the green sea,
Murmuring, craves their company,
Drawing the mist's long quivering quilt
Over each leaf-shaped wave.

Now in this season of the crying heart
Grief turns to find in the snowfall of leaves
A second dying of the dead, who start
In this their season from their quietude,
Rustling sadly their long, trailing sleeves.

ROY McFADDEN was born in Belfast in 1921 and now practises as
a solicitor. He has written in all five books of poetry, the most recent
being *The Garryowen* (1971) and *Verifications* (1977). He was co-editor
with Barbara Hunter of the Ulster journal of poetry, *Rann* which was
published from 1948 to 1953.

IN THIS THEIR SEASON   Roy McFadden   *March 1945*

WATER

By PEARSE HUTCHINSON

The sword of the sun is white on the water;
fire sparks out of it, sprays the poplar-green.
This marine and somber splendor makes tawdry
Wisping mauve clouds.

This flaring loveliness of the fluent sea
reminds me of others akin, different:
young, lisping laughter of a mountainy stream
Flipping the furze:

The falling over cataracts: the filling
a valley: the falling from asperges
of angels in astral cathedrals; the spilling
And ranting of rain;

On a red roof, the furious fingers of Mór
are tom-toms ten times quickened; soft-singing
harps for Lir's minstrelsy to pluck are the plashes
On amber-waved shore;

Look, in the park, the fountain is dancing
Ribbons of lace and froth; and foam-bandanas
are the raiment – like a sleek seal at the circus
It balances a ball;

Sharply the white efflorescence of ocean
bashes and busses the rocks. Crossing to the island
the boisterous water makes brief, gleaming, glass bangles,
As I feather my oar.

PEARSE HUTCHINSON was born in Glasgow in 1927 and brought to Ireland in 1932. *Water* was his first poem printed in *The Bell* in March 1945. Since then he has written poetry in English and Irish and translated it from the Catalan. His chief works in English are *Tongue Without Hands* (1963) and *Expansions* (1969).

WATER   Pearse Hutchinson   *March 1945*

THE LUCKY COIN

By AUSTIN CLARKE

Collect the silver on a Sunday,
Weigh the pennies of the poor.
His soul can make a man afraid
And yet thought will endure.
But who can find by any chance
A coin of different shape
That never came from Salamanca
Or danced on chapel plate^

Though time is slipping through all fingers
And body dare not stay,
That lucky coin, I heard men tell it,
Had glittered once in Galway
And crowds were elbowing the spirit
While every counter shone,
Forgetting grief until the ages
Had changed it for a song.

Turning in cartwheels on the fairground,
The sun was hastier —
That strolling girls might have for dowry,
Two hands about a waist;
Men voted for the Liberator
After the booths were closed
And only those in failing health
Remembered their own souls.

On Nephin many a knot was tied,
The sweet in tongue made free there,
Lovers forgot on the mountain-side
The stern law of the clergy
That kiss, pinch, squeeze, hug, smack denied,
Forgot the evil, harm
And scandal that come closer, lying
In one another's arms.

Not one of us will ever find
That coin of different shape
For it was lost before our rising
Or stolen — as some say.
But when our dream of the unseen
Has rifled hole and corner,
How shall we praise the men that freed us
From anything but thought.

AUSTIN CLARKE was born in 1896 and lived for most of his boyhood in Mountjoy Street which runs from Berkeley Road to St. Mary's Chapel of Ease, that dark building that gave him the title for his autobiography, *Twice Round the Black Church* (1960). He was educated at Belvedere and UCD. He is perhaps the greatest Irish poet after Yeats, though Patrick Kavanagh runs him so close that there is bound to be endless argument. His knowledge of Gaelic poetry and the great store of Irish literary tradition added to a polychromatic view of his countrymen makes his work whether retrospective or satirical a gaudy feast. His novels, verse and prose dramas convey the same sense of partaking at a banquet of marvellous richness. 'A Lucky Coin' is a very characteristic piece, lively, mysterious and sighing for a return of the spirit lost at the Famine. He died in 1974 shortly before his Collected Poems were published.

SIGNING OFF

By SEAN O'FAOLAIN

WITH this number *The Bell* passes to a new editor, or rather, more accurately, from one old campanologist to another since Peadar O'Donnell has been the Managing Editor since the inception of the magazine. The present writer has been editor for the last eleven volumes, and it is high time he moved on. He must, inevitably, have said by this most of the things he has to say; I am eager to return to my own proper literary pursuits; and, as perhaps most of our writers will agree, it would be a pleasant change to hear a more optimistic note, at any rate a less pessimistic one, than I have felt compelled to sound during these years. I have, I confess, grown a little weary of abusing our bourgeoisie, Little Irelanders, chauvinists, puritans, stuffed-shirts, pietists, Tartuffes, Anglophobes, Celtophiles, *et alii hujus generis.*

As I look back at the rows of issues which have had to bear my name I am surprised to find myself suddenly grown detached and impersonal about them. As I take them down and glance through them I begin to see all the mistakes we made at the start, and I see again all the things we might have done or wanted to do, and did not or could not. And when all is said and done, what I am mainly left with is a certain amount of regret that we were born into this thorny time when our task has been less that of cultivating our garden than of clearing away the brambles.

This did seriously intend, eleven volumes back, to be 'A Magazine of Creative Fiction'. We found that that was wishful thinking. We said that Life would stamp its own character on our venture and it has done so. We could not, and nobody could, or can, produce a purely literary or artistic magazine in

Ireland to-day — a magazine as full of poetic visions of ideal life, noble theories, interesting aesthetic ideas as Yeats, say, put into *Samhain,* and later into his autobiographical and critical books like *Hodos Chameliontos,* thirty or forty years ago. Indeed Yeats would not much care for this magazine (and I should not blame him), where politics and social problems intrude, and there is much that he would think purely on 'the surface of life'. It may be that as he did — and was sorry for it — we have gone too much into the arena, come too close to the battle. It may be that poetic truth, which lives remote from the battle, is more to be sought for than political truth. It may be, and one hopes so, that somewhere some young poet, scornful of us and our controversies, has been tending in his secret heart a lamp which will, in the end, light far more than can ever do — just as when other controversialists were hammering their public anvils aloud in his day, he, and his associates, were tending their secret lamps that lit a great resurrection here thirty years ago. All I can say is that our pages were and are open to all men of goodwill, and that we have worked hard and will keep on working hard to lure every writer to speak through these pages to Ireland. Besides, it is one thing to have a noble vision of life to come and another to have to handle what does come.

If, on this six years' experience, I had any hope to express for the future of Irish writing, whether it be writing of the day, journalism, or timeless writing, and for *The Bell,* which is the main vehicle of both to-day, it could, in fact, be expressed — not wholly, for I would not go the whole way with him — in Yeats' words about the arts being at their greatest 'when they seek for a life growing always more scornful of everything that is not itself'. When I spoke a moment ago of men of goodwill I implied a prohibition also — on men of evil will: and these we have assailed at every turn, partly because we felt that but for them there would be much more of that sort of writing in Ireland to-day which Yeats praised. To me, and so it must be to every artist — I will frankly say it, giving my last obstinate mule's kick — men like our present politicians are not men of goodwill because, in their hearts, they do not love life that 'passes into its own fullness'. And our censorious people are other haters of life that 'passes into its own fullness', and so are our pietists and chauvinists, puritans and the rest of all that tire-

some crew — being men in whose hearts there is none of that
poetry that

calls out in joy
Being the scattering hand, the bursting pod,
The victim's joy among the holy flame,
God's laughter at the shattering of the world.

We here have, as for the arts, been able (that is, dared in the
times in which we live) to ask for only one thing — that our
young writers should write of what they know. That means
that they must disabuse their minds of all the specious tempta-
tions with which our pimping moralists and pseudo-patriots
have beset the path of life in our time; they must, in Mauriac's
words, 'purify the source' of art, i.e. themselves, so that they
shall not write of what they are bid see but of what they do
see, not of what they are tempted to conceal but what their
hearts cry out to them to reveal, not of what floats the air-
filled balloons which our system of maleducation calls a mind
to-day (such as The Gaelic Mind, or the Catholic Mind, or the
Irish Mind), but of what the hawk in the air strikes in its flight.
If each writer will truly write of what *he* — a real and not a
false 'he' — *knows* — really knows and not pretends or is
deceived into 'knowing', then the rest is with God. Imagination,
vision, poetry, beauty — these attend the birth, or do not as
God decides. All the writer can do is to win personal honesty —
the hardest of all human achievements, in that fight with
himself of which Yeats again said: 'We lose our freedom more
and more as we get away from ourselves', and, 'We make of the
quarrel with others, rhetoric, but of the quarrel with ourselves,
poetry' — that fight in which nobody can help us, neither priest
nor statesman nor poet, nor anybody but our own daemon.
So, at times, people have made fun of our factual pieces, as on
a Rabbiting, or a Weasel, or a Spider, or a Pawnshop, or a
Ploughing-match: but we say — 'It is the beginning; if a man will
describe his own field faithfully, and pursues the search for
Truth from the field to the path, and the path to the house, and
the house to the hearth, and keep his courage, he will sooner or
later come to himself, and there the real fight will begin.' So,
we had a piece here a couple of years ago called 'Myself and
Some Ducks', and a few months ago 'Myself and Some Rabbits',

and they seemed to me to be the parable of the heart's search for the heart. That is all we have brought, in this little magazine, to modern Ireland.

We would wish that we had more articles on literature, and on aesthetics, and technique; and now that the War is over and the world opening up, we hope too that the Ireland beyond the seas will come to us; for we are a Mother Country; and a parochial Ireland, bounded by its own shores, has no part in our vision of the ideal nation that will yet come out of this present dull period. If that enlargement can take place, and with it a wider range of interests comes to be treated here, as the preoccupations and personal interests of our writers may decide, *The Bell* will move towards the fullness of its own life.

'SIGNING OFF' was written in April 1946 exactly six and a half years after *The Bell's* beginnings. It took the opportunity to evaluate the work of the magazine, to restate its purpose: 'epater' not only the bourgeoisie but also the other begrudgers of full life to the country, 'Little Irelanders, chauvinists, puritans, stuffed shirts, pietists, Tartuffes, Anglophobes, Celtophiles, *et alii hujus generis*'. It had hoped for an enlargement of Ireland's too parochial vision and now after some indication of widening it had the satisfaction of knowing that it had played no small part in this enlargement.

SIGNING OFF   Sean O'Faolain   *April 1946*

CAROL

By LOUIS MacNEICE

To end all carols, darling,
To end all carols now,
Let us walk through the cloister
With a thoughtful brow.

Pruning what was grafted
Through ages of blind faith—
The rubrics and the finials
Drift away like breath.

From Bethlehem the sheep-bells
Grew to a steepled peal,
The joists of the stable
Spread an ashlar chill,

The rafters of the stable
Hooped themselves on high
And coveys of boys' voices
Burst on a stone sky;

While the wrinkled, whimpering image
Wrapped in his mother's shawl
Was carried between pillars
Down endless aisles and all

The doors opened before him
In every holy place
And the doors came to behind him,
Left him in cold space.

Beyond our prayers and knowing,
Many light-years away—
So why sing carols, darling?
To-day is to-day.

Then answered the angel:
To-day is to-day
And the Son of God is vanished
But the sons of men stay.

And man is a spirit
And symbols are his meat,
So pull not down the steeple
In your monied street.

For money chimes feebly,
Matter dare not sing—
Man is a spirit,
Let the bells ring.

Ring all your changes, darling,
Save us from the slough;
Begin all carols, darling,
Begin all carols now.

LOUIS MacNEICE was born in Belfast 'between the mountains and the gantries' in 1907, the son of a nationally minded Church of Ireland clergyman who afterwards became Bishop of Down, Connor and Dromore. The account of his own life in *The Strings are False* (1965) shows a man of great tenderness, humour and fragility. He lectured in Greek at Birmingham University and afterwards joined the BBC Features Department under the legendary Laurence Gilliam. He was one of the finest poets of his generation reflecting the liberal conscience and defending the rights of the individual when the fascism of the Thirties and Forties seemed certain to sweep them away. His Irishness was recurrent and formal but the umbilical link was never severed. As he said in his poem 'Valediction', 'The woven figure cannot undo its thread'. He was poetry editor of *The Bell* in 1946 and 1947. He died of pneumonia in 1963.

CAROL   *Louis MacNeice*   *December 1946*

THE MIRROR

By MONK GIBBON

The rain falls in the mirror,
The mirror hangs on the wall,
And I look away from the window
And watch the rain fall.

Green branches, a veil of raindrops,
A drift of smoke, and some sky,
Glimpsed through thick leaves, this only
Twice-framed, is what meets the eye.

And I think, is this the fable
Of life as we know it now,
A room where we watch reflections,
Suspect the tree and the bough,

See them rain-laced but never
Completely revealed to sight,
Mantelshelf, mirror, window,
Rain, branches and then some light?

I lie on my bed reading,
Look up at that frame small,
The rain falls in the mirror,
The mirror hangs on the wall.

MONK GIBBON was born in Dublin in 1896 and educated at St. Columba's, Rathfarnham and Keble College, Oxford. He served in the RASC for the last two years of the Flanders War. He has written poetry, prose (including some excellent autobiography novels) and books upon film and architecture. One of his best known books is a non-adulatory account of his relations with Yeats, *The Mask and the Man* (1959). His unselfish work in shaping the great drift of paper left by Michael Farrell helped make the resulting work, *Thy Tears Might Cease* (1963) one of the great fiction successes of the post-war period in Ireland. 'The Mirror' was written during a visit to Belfast.

THE MIRROR   *Monk Gibbon*   *June 1947*

URCHINS
By RICHARD KELL

Patched trouser-seats and legs
pegged like washing along the parapet,
for a moment have been discarded
by eyes that are small blue whirlpools
greedily drinking the rhythm of boys
who slit the amber of the canal
like ivory paper-knives.

They chatter away like froth
from their tiny shoulders. Their secret is still unguessed—
a stagnant plash in the gloom
of those tenement skulls; square sockets
suck this glee to the cynical mirrors
that shape a face scooped out with pain...
These are the merry tragedians.

RICHARD KELL was born in Co. Cork in 1927. A graduate of TCD he became a full-time teacher in 1960 and is now a senior lecturer in English at Newcastle-upon-Tyne Polytechnic. His published work includes two collections of poetry: *Control Tower* (1962) and Differences (1969) but much of his work is uncollected. He is also a noted composer whose musical compositions have been performed by the Liverpool Philharmonic, the Northern Sinfonia and several BBC regional orchestras. A widower since 1975 he has four children. 'Urchins' is a typical urban idyl – a scene still common in summer along the Dublin canals although the 'tenements skulls' are fleshier now.

URCHINS   *Richard Kell*   *October 1947*

'TOO IMMORAL FOR ANY STAGE'
By ROGER McHUGH

IN Kilkenny in 1793 a poster which advertised a production of the tragedy of *Hamlet* by 'his Majesty'c Company of Comedians' was displayed. If one had not the authority of the *Kilkenny Archaeological Journal* for its authenticity one might be excused for believing it to have been an amusing fake. *Hamlet* was attributed not to Shakespeare, but to 'the celebrated Dan Hayes of Limerick'. Mr. Kearns, who was to take the principal part, was billed as performing between the acts 'several solos on the patent bag-pipes which play two tunes at the same time'. Mrs. Prior, in the part of Ophelia, said the poster, would 'introduce several favourite airs in character, particularly *The Lass of Richmond Hill* and *We'll All be Unhappy Together* from the Rev. Mr. Dibdin's Oddities'. It was announced further that the value of the tickets would be taken if required in candles, soap, butter, cheese, etc., as Mr. Kearns wished, in every particular, to accommodate the public; and that no person whatever would be admitted into the boxes without shoes or stockings.

But perhaps the prize item in this incredible poster was a special announcement:

'The parts of the King and Queen, by direction of the Rev. Father O'Callaghan, will be omitted, as too immoral for any

stage'...

That was over 150 years ago; yet within the past two years in theatrical circles in Dublin the mentality of this type of censorship appears to have reasserted itself. In 1946 a very reputable amateur dramatic society, the Athlone Little Theatre Group, entered Sean O'Casey's *Juno and the Paycock* for the Father Mathew Feis. The entry was rejected as 'not suitable for production'. To the Group's further enquiries as to the reason for this decision, the answer was returned that it was the duty of the Capuchin Fathers to pass all scripts entered for the Feis, that the Rev. President was mainly responsible, and that in the case of *Juno* nearly one whole act, as well as occasional lines, would have to be cut. One can only conjecture as to which act was considered unsuitable, but it seems probable that it was the act in which the seduction of Juno's daughter by the crooked solicitor Bentham forms part of the pattern of despair and darkness against which the figure of the mother stands out so nobly and with such genuine Christianity.

It seems particularly probable in view of certain events of this year, which began when the Athlone Little Theatre Group entered for the same Feis Gerard Healy's play *The Black Stranger*. This time the script was returned with a list of cuts which would have to be made if the entry was to prove acceptable to the Feis authorities. The list included a number of words (damn, God, begod, bloody), a number of isolated lines, and the whole scene in the second act which deals with Bridie's sacrifice of her virtue for a bag of meal to keep life in her starving household. This scene, like the scene dealing with the seduction of Juno's daughter, is a finely-written human scene depicting part of the tragedy which befalls a family. As played throughout long runs in Cork and in Dublin by the Players' Theatre Company it was deeply moving. The Athlone Group refused to omit and the author refused to allow them to cut it. Hence for the second year in succession a reputable amateur company was refused admission to the Father Mathew Feis on the grounds that the play entered was unsuitable.

Piquancy, as they say, was added to the situation by the fact that *The Black Stranger* had already won high praise at the Cavan Festival from Most Rev. Dr. Lyons, Bishop of Kilmore. The Tuam Players, who presented it there, were awarded the Dr. Lyons cup, and the actress who played Bridie won the medal for the best individual actress at the Festival. This was

pointed out by the Group to the authorities of the Father
Mathew Feis who were asked that in fairness to entrants a list
of the plays, authors and subjects to which they were likely to
object should be included in the syllabus of the Feis. They
replied that the standards of other festivals did not concern
them; 'The Father Mathew Festival has standards distinct
among dramatic festivals in Ireland and these we, at all costs,
endeavour to maintain'. The suggestion about the syllabus
was dismissed as impracticable and it was stated that 'a careful
examination of any play in the light of Christian ethics should
be sufficient to convince a competent producer regarding the
suitability or otherwise of any particular play for presentation
on a Catholic stage'.

The only part of this reply which appears to be tenable is
that which states that the Father Mathew Festival has standards
distinct among Irish dramatic festivals and that its authorities
are determined at all costs to preserve them. But what sort of
standards are they? If a play is to be barred because it includes
the dramatic treatment of seduction, if it is to be condemned
on that count as too immoral for any Catholic stage, are not
these standards simply the standards of the Rev. Father
O'Callaghan of Kilkenny in 1793? And are they worth preserv-
ing?

Whatever standards they are, they cannot be defended by
lofty references to Christian ethics and the Catholic stage. In
1937 when the Catholic University in Washington was planning
dramatic productions, it was urged to encourage 'Catholic
drama'. The American Catholic periodical *The Star* describes
the reaction of Father Hartke, the guiding spirit of the
University's drama department:

'Father Hartke and his associates felt that there were certain
discrepancies in this approach to the theatre. First of all, what
was a "Catholic play"? One written by a Catholic? One dealing
with a point of Catholic belief? And would a "Catholic drama"
rule out Sophocles, a pagan Greek, for instance? Would it rule
out Moliere, who died under an ecclesiastical cloud? Or
Christopher Marlowe, who professed atheism?... It seemed
reasonable to assume that the practice of the art of the theatre
for theatrical ends was a worthy work and one that might,
in its own small measure, contribute to the glory of God.'

That seems to me to display a sane sense of Christian ethics and to face honestly the question of the 'Catholic stage.' The present policy of some Capuchin Fathers in stage matters, on the other hand, seems to me to be likely to undo much good work for the amateur theatre in the past by using a fake conception of Christian ethics to defend a narrow and misguided censorship. The main hope of Irish drama, I believe, lies in the amateur little-theatre groups of Ireland and in their encouragement to present plays of merit, whether old or new. And all of them should be concerned with any attempt to make them play *Hamlet* without the King and Queen.

ROGER McHUGH was born in Dublin in 1908 and has been a member of the staff of UCD since 1930. He is now professor of English Literature. His historical contributions include *Henry Grattan* (1936) and *Carlow in Ninety-Eight* (1949). He has also been interested in Irish theatre with two plays to his credit: *Trial at Green Street Court House* (1941) and *Rossa* (1945). He and Valentin Iremonger took part in a mild protest in November 1947 against the Abbey Theatre's management policy. 'Too Immoral for any Stage' was published the same month and may serve as a reminder of the extremes to which censorship may go. The play in question has since become a regular favourite with even clerically run amateur drama societies.

'TOO IMMORAL FOR ANY STAGE'   *Roger McHugh*   *November 1947*

A GLIMPSE OF KATEY

By MARY LAVIN

KATEY felt drowsy all afternoon, so, shortly after supper, which had been a light one for the heart of the day had lessened her usual hunger, she decided that she would lie down, and that if she fell asleep she would not come downstairs any more, but stay in her room for the night.

'You'll be hungry before morning, Katey,' said her mother. 'You ought to bring up a glass of milk and a few biscuits, and leave them beside your bed in case you waken in the night.'

'I won't waken,' said Katey. 'I feel as if I could sleep for a week,' and she shuddered with distaste at the thought of eating another crumb, now, during the night, or indeed ever again.

'No matter how tired you are, you won't sleep if you're hungry,' said Katey's mother.

But Katey flounced out of the room, for although young people may listen to the voice of experience discoursing upon weighty matters of conduct or morality, about which their own ideas are vague and fearful, when it comes down to accepting peremptory advice upon such small matters as the tying of bow-knots, the plaiting of pig-tails, or the need for taking biscuits to bed, all that Youth will do is flounce its skirts and depart in the way that Katey did.

When Katey lay down the window panes were still bright with daylight, and the tops of the elm trees in the garden were plainly to be seen without raising the head from the pillow.

In the elms the birds were making preparations for the night; circling around the tree tops as if about to settle there, and then darting away again capriciously to take a last flight in the glowing clouds. But each time the flock circled down on the trees a number of birds settled there for the night, and every time they flighted away again there were less and less of them, until soon only one or two rose from the branches, and these only ventured a short distance, and came back with nervous fluttering and a great amount of nervous chirping.

When the last bird seemed to have settled down, and the leaves were no longer fluttered by shaken wings there was silence everywhere, except for occasional faint and single notes that broke the air at random and which seemed to come from the sleepy throat of some sleepy bird already hovering the air of dreams. Katey lay and listened, and then her own day suddenly slipped away from her, and left her body lying on the old four-poster bed, as the feathered bodies of the birds clung upon the damp tree-boughs, while her spirit with theirs was gliding away into the branchy lands of dream.

It was very dark when Katey woke up. The pale window pane that had reflected the bright trees was now dull and the branches of the trees were black as iron. Where the treble note of a bird had filled the air, there was the low bass note of the wood owl and the plaintive squeal of the flitter-mouse. And in the sky where the noisy birds had flown in companionable groups, there were motionless stars, cold and fixed; silent as death.

Katey put her hand out over the coverings and lay looking up at the stars. They were stern and forbidding. She pressed her face into the pillow again and tried to go to sleep once more.

It was no use. She could not sleep. And she was forced at last to admit to herself that she was very, very hungry, and that a biscuit − even a nibble of biscuit − would have satisfied her, if only she had one at hand. Her mother was right. She was wrong. And this fact, added to the fact that she was hungry, and the further fact that because she was hungry she could not go to sleep again, made Katey so unhappy that when she looked up at the stars a second time, they seemed to be splintered like broken glass, with long jagged points radiating to each side of them. A tear ran down Katey's left cheek, and it ran slowly and coldly because she lay flat on her back.

Katey thought of the food that had been on the table at supper, and which she had passed to Ruth and Mary without even glancing at it herself. She thought of the great cake that had been cut in two halves and in which the currants and candied fruits were as numerous as ink spots on a blotter, and she wondered how much of it had been eaten. She thought about the big bowl of prunes that was left on the sideboard, and the fat jug of milk that was refilled by Ellen the maid, whenever it showed the least signs of getting empty. And she wondered if this food was left on the sideboard all night. It would be worth going downstairs to investigate.

But as Katey put her foot out on the cold floor she thought of the long cold passage that lay between her and the stairs, and she thought of the stairs themselves with their great banister-rails that threw such shadows on the wall when you had only a candle to light your way. And she thought of the strange silence of the downstairs rooms, where in the absence of living people the pieces of furniture took on a character of their own, and the wicker chairs creaked, the dead embers gave out crackling sounds and the floor-boards gave out sudden sharp sounds of splitting wood. She pulled her foot back into bed again. The journey was too fearful to embark upon alone.

Thinking about the silence and loneliness of the house made Katey nervous, and she began to look distrustfully into the corners of her own room. Was the chest of drawers always as big as it seemed now in the darkness? And what was that shadow under the window? She was just going to sit up in bed to investigate when, in the corner farthest from her bed, she began to imagine that she had seen something move!

Her heart seemed to stop and then it began to beat again so furiously that she was afraid the bed would shake with the vibration. She stayed as still as she could stay and hardly dared to breathe.

And then, just as she had reached a point at which she would have to let her breath escape with a rush, to her astonishment, somewhere quite near she heard a voice saying something gay and brief, and then she heard several people laughing, and clapping their hands.

Katey sat up at once. She forgot the troublesome contours of the chest of drawers in the starlight. She forgot the bats that flew by the windows. She sat up and listened intently.

The voices came from downstairs, and they were the voices of her mother and her sisters. Once or twice there was a note struck on the piano and Gyp the terrier gave a bark. After the bark there was always a burst of laughter and the sound of clapping. Katey herself laughed in the dark. She knew just what was happening. Gyp disliked music of any kind, and one note on the piano was enough to make him cock his head and glare up fiercely with his small bright eyes at the underside of the keyboard where the notes moved stiffly up and down, marking time to the sounds they made like a soldier doing the goose-step.

It could not be as late as she thought. The others were still downstairs.

And jumping out of bed, Katey ran to the window and saw below on the lawn the bright reflections of the drawing-room windows, and in them she saw the shadow of the little dog, with one ear up and one ear down.

She must go down and join in the fun. Katey dragged her dressing jacket over her shoulder and pulled the cord of the belt around her waist so tight that she was almost severed in two like an hour-glass. Then she opened the door of her bedroom and ran out into the passage.

As Katey ran down the passage her slippers flapped on the floor and when she shook her head and tossed back her long hair over her shoulder it struck against the wallpaper to either side of her in the way the pony's tail flipped against the tilt of the cart when he wanted to scatter the flies that stung him. But Katey was unaware that she was making any noise and when the door of her father's room opened and her father put out his head, Katey was so surprised that she stopped up dead in the middle of a stride.

'What is the meaning of all this noise I hear?' her father demanded, and he stepped out into the passage himself and began to fasten the cord of his dressing gown with much the same determination with which Katey had fastened hers a moment before.

'What noise, Father?' said Katey and she pulled in to the marginal boards at the side of the carpet-strip as a cyclist pulls in to the kerb when a superior vehicle approaches with a view to passing it out while proceeding in the same direction.

'Need you ask?' said her father as there was a resounding chord struck upon the piano in the room below followed immediately by the frantic bark of a dog, which was in its turn followed by such peals of laughter that those who uttered them could hardly be supporting themselves upright, but must assuredly be sprawled in abandon upon the couches and chairs.

'This is a nice hour of the night for music and barking!' said Katey's father. 'Who could sleep with noise like this going on? Women have no consideration. Your mother and sisters can lie in bed all day but I have to get up for my work... I've told your mother a thousand times if I don't get to sleep in the early part of the night I don't sleep at all, and if I lose a night's sleep I'm fit for nothing the next day.' He pulled his tasselled cord tighter. 'What time is it?' he asked.

But just at that moment the clock on the landing struck the hour, and together the two figures at the head of the stairs began to count the strokes, unconsciously nodding their heads at each stroke, and beginning to stare at each other with widening eyes as the strokes became more and more numerous.

'Twelve o'clock!' said Katey's father, and he began to cough, as if the lateness of the hour had reminded him of the dampness and coldness of the passage which he had not noticed before.

'Hhrrr. Hhrrr!'

When Katey's father coughed he kept his mouth shut from politeness, but his jowls swelled up and shook, and the noise that came forth from his nostrils resembled the neigh of a horse. When he had coughed a sufficient number of times, Katey's father fixed his eye once more on the face of the clock.

'No normal person would be out of his bed at this hour!' He advanced to the head of the stairs and leaned over the banisters as if he was about to roar down to those below. But on second thoughts he turned around suddenly upon Katey. 'What are you doing out of your bed at this hour?' he said.

Katey trembled. She gazed with fright into her father's angry eye and was absolutely unable to look away again, and absolutely unable to give him any reply.

'What were you doing here in the passage when I came out? Were you going down to join the others?'

Below, there was another note struck upon the piano, another bark and another burst of uncontrollable laughter. This time it seemed louder than ever, and Katey trembled more violently in proportion.

'Answer me,' cried her father and he could hardly hear himself above the din.

Katey hesitated for one moment and then she answered him in a rush.

'They woke me too, Father! I couldn't sleep with the noise.'

Her father relaxed.

'That's what I thought,' he said. 'Poor child. You take after me. You have some sense. You need an unbroken sleep. Get back to bed. I can assure you there will be no more noise tonight,' and giving his tasselled belt a final tug till it disappeared in the depths of the dressing gown, he leaned over the banisters and roared down into the rooms below with such a rumble of anger that although Katey heard what he said it is possible that those below could hear only the thunderous roar of disapproval.

'What do you mean by this noise?' cried Katey's father. 'This is no hour for piano playing. If you had any respect for yourselves, or consideration for others, you'd be in your beds long ago. Disgraceful! Disgraceful!'

The last two words fell upon the air like the heavy notes of the big standing clock in the hall, and after them, like the thin notes of a small enamel clock, came Katey's voice.

'Disgraceful! Disgraceful!' said Katey, and she scampered back in front of her father along the upper passage, and ran into her room and sprang into bed, and this time her heart beat so loud that she tried to hold it still with her hands.

Very soon she heard footsteps outside her door, and low nervous giggling.

'Are you awake, Katey?' said a voice, close to the key-hole, but, more alert than the gigglers, Katey could hear the springs of the bed groan under her father's weight in the room on the other side of the wall, and she pressed her lids down tightly over her eyes and pretended not to hear. She pretended to be asleep, but she felt no comfort when the footsteps moved away, causing a loose board to creak, and accompanied by more muffled laughing, because she knew that she could not pretend to be asleep in the morning, and that then she would have to go downstairs and meet them all, and look them in the eyes.

Around the room the shadows grew to greater bulk than before, and lurked in every corner, but Katey was not afraid of them. She was only afraid of the morning.

MARY LAVIN was born in Walpole, Massachusetts in 1912, the only daughter of Thomas Lavin of Roscommon and Nora Mahon of Athenry. She was taken to Ireland in 1921 and finally settled in Bective, Co. Meath in 1926. Her first book *Tales from Bective Bridge* was published in 1942, the year of her marriage to William Walsh. Since then she has written many other books and become Ireland's leading woman writer, famous for the particular excellence of her short stories. The death of her husband in 1954, not unnaturally interfered with her output but since 1956 she has kept up a steady flow of superior stories. Over the years she has been the recipient of the James Tait Black Memorial Prize, the Kathfield Mansfield Prize, the Ella Lynam Cabot Award and two Guggenheim Fellowships. Her descriptions of love, death and living in quiet desperation are relieved by humour and a deep knowledge of the spiritual and economic drives of her mainly rural characters. Her stories are local and except in flights of imagination generally unexotic. The virtues she most admires are the ones she writes about: emotional control, forbearance and patience, in settings where these words still have meaning. She married Michael MacDonald Scott, Dean of the School of Irish Studies in 1969 and the family divides its time between Dublin and Bective. 'A Glimpse of Katey', one of two short stories printed in *The Bell* is a gentle but precisely observed incident in the life of a growing girl.

A GLIMPSE OF KATEY   Mary Lavin   *November 1947*

BUCHENWALD

By DENIS JOHSTON

AS I drove through the woods the trickle of Displaced Persons grew in volume, until presently there was a continual stream of them — filthy, emaciated creatures, many of them in those disgusting striped pyjamas in which the S.S. clothe their internees. The concrete road and the railway track were easy to find, and as I bowled down the former I passed a bombed-out factory, and then found myself confronted by a great gate in a barbed wire fence surmounted by a large black flag. An American sentry kept watch over an enormous pile of rifles, machine guns and other weapons that had been collected by the side of the road, and the D.P.s were milling around on both sides of the fence.

'Say, what's this place?' I asked the sentry.

As usual he didn't know, except that it was some Concentration Camp that had been overrun by Patton's boys, and that
the D.Ps were still hunting the S.S. guards in the woods and
lynching them. Indeed if I cared to look in any of the ditches...

'Would you like to see over the camp an English voice
enquired at my elbow.

I turned around and found myself facing two internees,
dressed in ragged clothes and holding under their arms bundles
wrapped in sacking.

'Thanks,' I said. 'Are you English?'

'Channel Islanders,' replied the first. He introduced himself
as James Quick and his friend as Emile Dubois.

'Come with us and we'll bring you round by the back. Have
you got a strong stomach?'

Over the main gate I read a defiant inscription:

RECHT ODER UNRECHT – MEIN VATERLAND.

So there had evidently been some doubt in somebody's mind
about the rightness or wrongness of this place! On an inner gate
a shorter and even more cynical inscription appeared: JEDEM
DAS SEINEM, or in a free translation, 'To each what is coming
to him.'

By this time I suspected what was coming to me, and I
steeled myself for another recital of uncorroborated horrors.
But my guides were not so talkative as they might have been.
They were bitter, it is true, on the subject of turnip soup and
one loaf of bread a day between five, but strangely enough,
they didn't complain so vigorously about their own lot. They
had been in a part of the camp that wasn't too bad, they said,
because they were still fit to work. But wait until I saw the
fate of those who weren't. At which Dubois stripped the corner
of a tarpaulin off a lorry that was standing in the yard, and
disclosed the interior piled high with emaciated yellow naked
corpses.

Like Alexander I have not seen many dead in the course of
this war: graves by the thousand, and lots of impersonal lumps
under covers; but the unsheeted dead have been limited to
those waxlike figures in the houses of Ortona and a few more

here and there by the roadside. I do not like looking on the dead — not that they move me, so much as disgust me. This was a sight in full measure, and I did not brood on it for long.

'Cover it up,' I said, 'and tell me how it happened?'

'It happens all the time,' Dubois answered. 'This is just a day or two's collection. Come and see inside.'

I had laughed off that camp in Alsace, and what they said of it, but I couldn't laugh this one off, for here it was obvious that most patent efforts had been made to conceal the evidence. In the cellar beneath the crematorium, somebody had been trying to whitewash the walls, but the bloodstains still showed up beneath the new colour. They had taken the hooks out of the walls above each gory splash and had attempted to fill up with plaster the holes that had been left. But the patches still remained, and one great hook had been restored, evidently for some last minute hanging. The stools were still there, and a dented and bloody bludgeon — a couple of the little short narrow nooses, and what to me was probably the most horrible of all — a white coat like that of a hospital attendant, half washed of the blood that had once engrained it.

'They beat us, and hanged us here,' said Quick.

And for all I might try, there was no denying the evidence.

'Come and see upstairs.'

Alsace was small time stuff compared to this. Instead of one furnace there were half a dozen, and in some of them the charred bones still lay.

'Don't mind those,' said my guide. 'They were put there by some of the prisoners to dress the place up a bit.'

'That seems scarcely necessary,' I answered, my stomach turning within me at the thought of such ghoulish deliberation.

'That's what I thought. But some people can't let bad alone. They've got to fix it up for the photographers.'

But if the prisoners were being business-like in their preparations, it was nothing to the neat organisation of the jailers. For here again I was not so much revolted by the fact of death — which must happen sooner or later, as by a painting of a hearty, flaming furnace on one of the end walls of the crematorium, surmounting an inscription that looked for all the world like a religious motto, or a Christmas greeting. But it did not say God Bless Our Home. It translated as follows: —

Not a horrible and distasteful warmth will feed upon my

corpse, but a clean fire will digest it. I always loved warmth
and light, therefore burn and do not bury me.

This was the jolly sentiment that was put into the mouths of
the wretches who had not died a natural death, but had been
beaten to death or hanged in the cellar down below.

'It's quite pretty here in the summer,' said Quick, as we
walked through the camp. 'They have a little concrete aquarium
just outside the wire there, and trees look nice, don't they?

'We even had a sort of band that used to play in the evenings
over by the gate. It really wasn't so bad — so long as you could
work.'

'And if you couldn't?'

'If you couldn't work, or if you got in bad with them, they
sent you down to the lower part of the camp.'

'And what happened there?'

'Would you like to come and see for yourself?'

'I fancy somehow that I would not. But I suppose that I had
better.'

'Come along then.'

We walked through the camp. Sub-human specimens were
tottering around on all sides as we went, most of them dressed
in those dreadful striped pyjamas, but all of them in a state of
indescribable filth. Many of them squatted over the open
drains with their pants down.

'Dysentry is the least serious complaint we have here,'
explained Dubois. 'It only begins with that.'

'But where did such people come from,' I asked.

'Oh, they were just ordinary people when they came here. In
fact most of them were quite well-off people before they fell
foul of the party. For instance, that one there was a throat
specialist in Vienna, and the one behind him was once the
Mayor of Prague, they say.'

'Tell me,' I said, feeling madly around for an explanation,
'this state of affairs isn't normal, of course. This congestion and
starvation is a result of the end of the war? — the breakdown
of life generally in Germany?'

'To some extent maybe. But it isn't much worse than usual.
Normally they kept 70,000 people here, and as soon as your
working ability was over, what followed was quite deliberate.
It doesn't take you long to get to that state at sixteen hours
work a day; and after you've collapsed physically you're just a

useless mouth. The sooner you're dead the better. It's a logical
Nazi idea. But surely you knew? Haven't you read their books?'

'Yes, I've read their books. But somehow... never mind, tell
me what happened when the Yanks got near? Why did they
leave you alive to talk?'

'They did their best, but 70,000 people take a bit of killing,
you know, and it isn't everyone will do it. As a matter of fact
on the 11th they mounted eight machine guns on the gate, and
we heard that a killer squad of 500 S.S. men had been sent from
Weimar to exterminate the camp. But the Yanks beat them to it
by two hours, and at about four in the afternoon we saw the
first tanks coming up. At that, the guards and their dogs ran for
the woods, and some of the boys have been hunting for them
since. In fact I'm afraid they've been beating up the whole
countryside.'

I didn't ask what happened to the S.S. men when they were
caught. I had seen signs myself, on the way up, and it was a
good killing.

'Here's the block we want you to see,' said Quick. 'Don't
come in if you don't want to.'

I went in. At one end lay a heap of smoking clothes amongst
which a few ghouls picked and searched — for what. God only
knows. As we entered the long hut the stench hit us in the face
and a queer wailing sound came to our ears. Along both sides
of the shed was tier upon tier of what can only be described
as shelves. And lying on these, packed tightly side by side, like
knives and forms in a chest, were living creatures — some of
them stirring, some of them stiff and silent, but all of them
skeletons, with the skin drawn tight over their bones, with
heads bulging and misshapen from emaciation, with burning
eyes and sagging jaws. And as we came in, those with the
strength to do so turned their heads and gazed at us; and from
their lips came that thin unearthly noise.

Then I realised what it was. It was meant to be cheering.
They were cheering the uniform that I wore. They were
cheering for the hope that it brought them.

We walked the length of the shed — and then through
another one. From the shelves feeble arms rose and waved, like
twigs in a breeze. Most of them were branded with numbers.

'Hoch—Hoch—Viva—Viva!'

*   *   *

Recht oder unrecht — mein Vaterland.

Through the gates, under this monstrous sentiment, the American Red Cross orderlies were trooping as we came out. As I bade farewell to my two guides one of them bent over the pile of captured weapons on the sidewalk and picked out a Luger.

'How about a souvenir?' he said.

The American sentry casually looked the other way. From the woods around us came the distant sound of a shot. Staring at the gateway and at the white helmets of the orderlies I took the gun and shoved it under my coat.

Recht oder unrecht.

American medicos on a mission in favour of the human race — for that is the issue here, and there is no getting away from it.

This is no fortuitous by-product of the chaos of war. This is no mere passing cruelty or wanton act of destruction. This is deliberate. This is the intentional flower of a Race Theory. This is what logic divorced from conscience can bring men to. This is the wilful dehumanisation of the species, and an offence against Homo Sapiens.

Right or wrong — my Fatherland.

Very well. Have it that way if you insist. Your Fatherland is wrong, therefore your Fatherland must be destroyed. That is logic too. Put it to the test, and if you lose — you must die.

Unconditional surrender is the only answer.

Oh, I have tried so long to fight against this conclusion, but now — as at the thirteenth stroke of a crazy clock — all previous pronouncements become suspect too. Everything else falls into place and acquires a new meaning in the hideous light of Buchenwald. The words of Winston Burdett — the million shoes of Lublin — that camp in Alsace that I laughed at, because I did not want to believe such things of men — because they were not true of men as I had known them.

Cruelty I have known, and sadism, and the villainy of red-hot anger. But mass de-humanisation as a matter of planned policy has not so far come my way.

Worse for me is the fact that I have been made a fool of, in my thirst for fairness and international justice. All the reasonable and sensible things that Hitler has ever said — the virtue of Courage and Order, the justice of self-determination and unity, the fact that we went to war to preserve Danzig for the

Poles, the evil of money power, the right of a great people to a place in the sun — all these things were just a cover-up for this!

He has been using our good nature as a means of betraying us; and that is even a greater crime than the degradation of humanity, for it is the degradation of Good itself. It means that Good is not worth while — that Evil is our only means of self-preservation, that like the Vampire, Dracula, he has bitten me upon the throat, and I must either die or be a monster too!

How did I ever dare to doubt that there was not an Absolute in Good and Evil?

And what else has he done? He has delivered us bound hand and foot into the power of the Prigs of Ill-will and from now on I am forced to be their ally. This camp will be their war-cry. They will seize upon it with the whoops of joy. They will all be here in a day or two, threading their way through its filth — no frozen horror or revulsion in their eyes — nothing but lust and self-righteousness. They will photograph and film it in prepared poses. They will blazon it to the skies as a justification for every crime that will be committed in return. Good nature, they will scream, is folly, and love of justice is only sentimentality. And they will have Buchenwald to prove them right, for all that they will say of Buchenwald is true — every word of it or nearly every word! Buchenwald has buggered up the Master Plan.

Oh Christ! We are betrayed. I have done my best to keep sane, but there is no answer to this, except bloody destruction. We must slay the Oxen of the Sun whatever the Gods may feel about it. We must break the double gates in pieces and fling down the walls, and whoever tries to stop us, be he guilty or innocent, must be swept aside. And if nothing remains but the stench of evil in ourselves, that cannot be helped!

How terrible that this should be the place that I have been seeking for all these years. I thought that it was Eckartsberga, but it seems that it was Buchenwald. And now, on this terrible — this unforgettable day — I have found it.

DENIS JOHNSTON was born in Dublin in 1901 and after an extensive formal education was called to the English Bar in 1925 and the Northern Ireland Bar in 1926. One of Ireland's major dramatists he made an immediate reputation with the then experimental play, *The Old Lady*

Says No! in 1926, a position confirmed by *The Moon in the Yellow River* (1931). He has worked in theatre (director of the Gate from 1931 to 1936), in radio and television. His preoccupation with the riddle of the life and personality of Jonathan Swift has produced some fascinating books and plays, particularly the attempt at biography, *In Search of Swift* (1959) and the play *The Mask of Polyphemus* (1958). He was a BBC war correspondent from 1942 to 1945 and out of these experiences he created one of his finest books, *Nine Rivers from Jordan* (1953) which is also one of the best books to come out of the war. This excerpt from his war diaries was later incorporated in the book and recalls his reaction to the discovery that the facts of the Nazi concentration camps far outpassed the wildest of the rumours.

He lives in Dalkey and is father of the novelist Jennifer Johnston.

BUCHENWALD   *Denis Johnston*   *March 1951*

THE STRANGE WOMAN
By DAVID MARCUS

I WAS very young at the time, the night my father brought a strange woman home and said, 'Billy, this is your new mother. Say 'hello' and give her a big kiss, she's your mother from now on.' He smiled awkwardly while the woman bent down and left me touch her cheek with my lips. Her skin was pale and cold, and I thought she was shivering a bit. I hadn't time to ask any questions because then my father said, 'Put your books away now, boy, and go up to bed.' I closed up my books and stuffed them into my sack even though I had not quite finished all my lessons — but I knew that by rushing breakfast next morning and getting to school a bit earlier than usual, I could finish them there. I always obeyed all my father's instructions; he used to say that was what my mother — my real mother — would have wanted and that she was always watching me. I did not know if he was right because I could not remember for myself what she looked like, so I always had to think of the photograph of her in the bedroom and pretend that that was what he meant.

I put my sack in a corner and walked towards the door. I must have been puzzled by the strange woman because I almost forgot to say 'good-night'. But at the door I suddenly remembered and turned, saying, 'Good-night, father,' as I did so. He must have forgotten also because he had his back to me and a hand on the woman's arm. He whirled quickly and said, 'Good-night, boy,' and then, prompting me, he added, 'And good-night, mother.' She opened her lips as if also to help me say it, but she just half-smiled and said nothing. I said 'Good-night, mother,' and went up to bed.

There were two bedrooms upstairs but I always slept in the front one with my father. We shared the big double-bed, opposite which stood that photograph of my mother on the mantelpiece. Now and again I went over to look at it, and this night I studied it for quite a while. In it she wore a plain, white frock that seemed to hang shapelessly on her body and she stood against a trellis that had roses massing through its diamond spaces and spilling over the top above her head. But it was a very poor photograph because her eyes were all puckered up from the sun, and the overhanging roses were so thick that they put the top of her head in shadow. All I could really see was that she had a long face and thin lips; and whether her hair was actually dark or not I could not be sure. I often wondered if it was my father who had taken the photograph, and where — it hadn't been taken in our garden because we never had a trellis or roses. A few times I had almost asked him to tell me but for some reason I always drew back at the last moment. I think I was happier not knowing anything about her — I felt she was more mine that way, for I could make her up to my own fancy. Anyway I don't think he would have told me even if I had asked him because, once, when he said that she was always watching me, I asked if she was always watching him, too, and he grew suddenly still and did not answer.

Slowly I began to undress myself, thinking about her and about my new mother. I know I didn't understand at the time what had happened, but I was also not conscious that there was anything much that had to be understood. It was just a change of conditions to me — a big change, of course — but all changes

had always been brought about by my father and I was used
to accepting them, big or small, without question or the need
to question.

I had got my clothes folded on the chair and my pyjamas
onto me when I heard my father run up the stairs. He rushed
into the bedroom, a bit flushed, and said, 'Oh, Billy, I forgot
to tell you. You're changing rooms. I'll help you move your
clothes into the other one. You'll be fine there, boy, eh?'
I took this change also in the same way as before and gathered
my clothes in a bundle into my arms while my father picked up
my boots and followed behind me. At the door he said, 'Wait
now,' went back to the mantelpiece for the photograph and
placed it on top of my bundle of clothes, saying, 'You'd better
take this, too, boy.' He said it quietly and smiled at me quietly.
When I got into the other room, he put my boots down, ruffled
his hand through my hair and then quickly left. The new room
was quite small, its walls and mantelpiece bare. I put the photograph on the mantelpiece and got into bed. I lay on my right
side so as I could see through the window into the yard of the
neighbour's house next door. Old 'Dodder', their cocker spaniel,
was lying there, half in and half out of his kennel. I don't know
how long I watched him or what I was thinking of, but I
remember he barked once, long and low, before I fell asleep.

Next day in school, during the history lesson, Jimmy
Drummond leant forward from the desk behind me, and
whispered in my ear, 'Your old man's got a new missus. I heard
my mum saying he's got a new missus.' I didn't turn around or
answer as the master was looking at me and he had been crusty
all morning. But anyway I had nothing to say because my new
mother had been still in bed when I went out to school. My
father had made breakfast for me and had spoken very little
besides asking if I liked sleeping alone. He had said that I must
get used to sleeping alone now because I would have to show
my new mother that I could be a man. I hadn't minded sleeping
alone and told him so. He laughed and gave me twopence. He
usually gave me only one penny every morning but he said that
if I was to be a man from now on, I'd have to get a man's wage.

I had forgotten what Jimmy Drummond had said until school
was over. But then he caught up with me as I was leaving and
shouted to the other boys, 'Hey, boys, Billy's old man has a
new missus. Hasn't he, Billy?' he added, turning to me. 'What's

she like?' questioned someone else, as they all gathered round.
'He got her from Hoxton's Fair. My sister told me that she was
working in a stall at Hoxton'. I was hemmed in by the gate.
Another boy laughed and whispered, 'I heard my folks say that
she was well known at the Fair, and my mum says it's a shame
and a sacrilege. What's she like, Billy? Does she do tricks like
the woman at the circus last summer?' There was a shout of
laughter at this and they all pushed at me, asking questions. I
hadn't answered at all — I was feeling frightened of them and
ashamed that I couldn't think of good answers to satisfy them
or make them stop laughing. Then Jimmy Drummond winked
at me and said, 'Takes your old man, Billy. He was always a
hard one.' For the first time in my life I felt completely lost,
completely unsure of things that I had only then realised were
of great importance. I couldn't think and I didn't understand.
I broke away from the boys and ran down the hill while they
all stood at the gate, laughing and shouting.

When I got home the strange woman opened the door for
me and Mrs. Ogilvie was not there at all. Mrs. Ogilvie was the
woman who always kept house for us and who used stay with
me till my father came home from work. I asked if she was
ever coming back again and my new mother said, 'No Billy,
I'll be here every day with you now. Come on, mummy has a
grand dinner for you.' She seemed much cheerier than the night
before but her skin was still pale. While I ate my dinner, she sat
down reading a newspaper and I kept stealing glances at her.
Her lips were painted heavily and her eyelashes were very long.
She had raven-black hair, flowing down on both sides from the
middle of her head like a black waterfall. She wore a black
dress, too, with a gold bangle around her neck and another on
her left wrist. Whenever she turned over the newspaper her
red nails flashed in the light.

They flashed that way very often because she became fidgety
and kept going back to pages she had read before. Sometimes
our looks would meet, and when they did she turned her head
away quickly. After a while she bent down to a black bag beside
her on the floor and took out a cigarette. When she had it lit
she became much quieter. I suppose she had wanted to smoke
all the time but was somehow afraid to do so in front of me.
But I didn't mind because Mrs. Ogilvie used smoke too. When I
finished my dinner she cleared the table, and asked me if I were

going to do my lessons. Usually I used wait till my father would come home and do them with me at night, but I thought that perhaps he had told her to make me do them after dinner, so I got out my books and started. She didn't help me but sat back with the newspaper and smoked many cigarettes.

For about a week things carried on like this. Each night my father came home from work he used send me to bed early, and I liked that because he started bringing me adventure books and allowed me to read them in bed. He was in great form for that week and my new mother would laugh now and again with him But mostly she said nothing, and it was his voice I would hear as I lay in bed, reading. They never once went out.

But then one night, after I had put out the light and was almost asleep, I suddenly realised that my father was shouting and I thought I could hear a woman's voice crying. My ears weren't awake enough to make out any words so I jumped out of bed to listen at the door. Immediately I did so my father's voice was hushed and the woman's sobs became lower as if they had both heard my feet on the floor. I crept back into bed, afraid my father might come up, and I fell asleep wondering why he had been shouting and why my new mother was crying.

Next day when I came home from school, it was Mrs. Ogilvie who opened the door to me. I was surprised to see her again, of course, and glad too, and she was overjoyed to see me. She bent down to throw her arms around me and squeezed me against her bulging bosom. My face sank into it until I was almost breathless and she kept rubbing the back of my head with her hands.

'The poor boy,' she was mumbling, 'the poor boy. Such a way to treat a youngster.'

By now the accumulation of surprises was beginning to exasperate me and I was no longer willing to accept them meekly. I asked Mrs. Ogilvie what she meant and what was wrong. But she only continued mumbling in a lower voice so that I could not distinguish the words, and she gave me no answer. I felt that if Mrs. Ogilvie wouldn't tell me, then nobody would, so I went in to my dinner. She had prepared almost every food I especially liked and stood over me, chugging like a barge, while I ate.

It was not till about eight o'clock that night that my father came home, and my new mother was with him. Mrs. Ogilvie could not leave till then, of course, and she was not happy at being delayed. We all stood in the kitchen while she had a few words with him about domestic matters, and then she prepared to go. My father mentioned, just conversationally, that she would be along again to-morrow and Mrs. Ogilvie replied that she would, but that she'd have to be out at her usual time of six-thirty. She seemed quite huffed. My father said nothing, while my new mother just gazed in front of her, looking very unhappy. Mrs. Ogilvie passed her on her way out but they did not speak to each other.

'Now, boy, up to bed with you,' said my father when she was gone. But that afternoon I had gone back to my ould routine and had postponed doing my lessons until my father would have returned to help me. When I told him that, he paused a moment, and then said, 'Never mind them now; it's too late. In the morning, I'll give you a note to the teacher.' Naturally this satisfied me, and I went to bed.

I was not long there when I heard him shouting and my new mother shouting back. This time I was wide awake and had made no mistake about it so I did not have to get out of bed to listen. The shouting went on for some time until suddenly they both stamped out to the hall. Then I heard the front door being opened and banged shut. My heart jumped at this — I thought I was left by myself in the house. But after a few seconds I heard my father's steps return alone to the room. I stayed awake as long as I could, clutching the pillow, but when I fell asleep my father had not yet come up to bed.

In the morning I had to mention to him twice about the note to the teacher. I could almost see him wrenching his brain around to deal with it and as he had forgotten what it was all about, I had to explain even that too. Then he scribbled it out quickly and sent me off.

All through school and the afternoon with Mrs. Ogilvie I was impatient for my father to come home, for I was now full of curiosity and, I suppose, in my own way, worried too. But at half-past six he had not returned. We waited till eight when Mrs. Ogilvie told me to go to bed. But I refused and said I would wait for my father and she did not insist. When he did come it was after ten, and he was alone. Immediately he saw me he snapped out, 'Why is the boy still up, Mrs. Ogilvie? Why didn't you put him to bed?' I had never heard him use such an

angry tone to us before and I timidly told him that I was
waiting for him to come home. He said nothing but just sat
down in a chair and sighed. Mrs. Ogilvie motioned to me to go
upstairs, so I went to bed. That was Friday night and as there
was no school again till Monday I did not have to worry about
my lessons.

Next day was the same except that my father came home a
bit earlier this time, though again my new mother was not with
him. He allowed me stay up a while when Mrs. Ogilvie left but
he did not speak to me at all. He just sat in his chair, gazing
ahead of him. At about nine o'clock he said, 'Good-night, Billy.
It's about time for you now,' and I went up.

Going to bed so late for two nights must have made me
sleepy for I did not wake up till eleven on Sunday morning, and
when I went down to breakfast Mrs. Ogilvie was there. This
had never happened before; usually on Sunday mornings my
father would do my lessons with me and then take me out in
the afternoon. I asked Mrs. Ogilvie where he was and she told
me that he had to go out but that he would be back as quickly
as possible. But I knew somehow that he'd be late again so I
did my lessons myself.

He *was* late, though not quite as much as I expected. When
he saw me he didn't seem to mind that I was not in bed, but he
sent me into another room while he spoke to Mrs. Ogilvie.
After about five minutes she opened the door to say 'good-
night' and told me that I could go back to my father. When I
did, he smiled at me, and then closed his eyes and put his head
back against the chair. His face was whiter than I had ever seen
it before and he was very tired. I could see that he was thinking
to himself and had forgotten about me. I was thinking, too;
thinking about my new mother in the black dress and wondering when she would be coming back. I kept gazing at my
father's face so much that suddenly I realised I was almost
falling asleep. It must have been very late by then so, without
making any noise or saying 'good-night', I crept up to bed.

I don't know how long I had been asleep when I was
awakened by someone pushing my shoulder. I opened my eyes
and saw my father looking down at me. 'Come on, boy,' he
whispered, 'you can come back to my bed again'. I yawned,
and asked him, 'Only for to-night, is it, daddy?' He didn't
answer this. He didn't have to: I knew myself it was not only

for the night, that this was the last change of all and that from now on we would go back to our old ways.

I tumbled out of bed while he gathered up my clothes and boots and led the way out. At the door he seemed about to stop and I sensed what he wanted. Quickly I ran back for the photograph of my mother and, clutching it tightly, followed my father once again.

DAVID MARCUS was born in Cork in 1924. He was educated in University College, Cork, and King's Inns, Dublin, and was called to the Bar in 1945. He was founder-editor of *Irish Writing* (1945-1954) and of Poetry Ireland (1948-1954). He published poems and stories in many periodicals and is the author of a novel. *To Next Year in Jerusalem* (1954) (the traditional toast at the end of the feast of Pesach). His is by far the liveliest translation of *The Midnight Court*. After an exile in London he returned to Dublin and began what has been the greatest outlet for new writers since the days of *The Bell* itself. *New Irish Writing*, which was ten years old in 1978. This important Irish institution appears each week in *The Irish Press* of which he is also Literary Editor. In recent years he has edited six anthologies of Irish short stories and *Irish Poets*, a collection of modern Irish verse.

THE STRANGE WOMAN   David Marcus   *April 1951*

A HALF-CROWN

By MICHAEL McLAVERTY

BEFORE dusk nine or ten over-excited boys were going round the houses in the street begging stuff for their annual Fifteenth-of-August bonfire. Anything at all would do they boldly announced to the neighbours: old boxes, oil-cloth, newspapers, broken chairs, and thrown-out mattresses – and they would point to the middle of the street where a miscellaneous heap of these articles was stacked as high as the arms of the lamp-post. In two hours time when the blue darkness of summer would slowly descend upon the street they would blacken or paint their faces, wear bowler hats and old garments, and sprinkling the heap with paraffin they would accompany the first bursts of flame by yelling a hymn in honour of the Blessed Virgin: then they would dance round the ring of flame, shouting and laughing, letting off fireworks, while their mothers and fathers gathered in an outer circle would encourage their wild Indian antics.

Now as they pressed eagerly round the doors they cheered when anything was handed out to them, and as they carried these objects shoulder-high or dragged them to the spreading pile they would cheer again and dash off once more, promising themselves that this would be the greatest bonfire that was ever seen in their district. Presently they reached the end-house of the street where an old woman lived alone; here they halted in a compact group, whispering and debating among themselves whether to rap the door or turn back. They feared this woman, for she was always muttering mysteriously to her self and seldom opened her door except to threaten them with the police or with a stick whenever they came to play handball against the gable of her house. But to-night their tense feelings had numbed their fear of her, and the biggest boy among them struck his chest stoutly and volunteered to knock the door even if no one else would venture with him. He stepped out from the group and rapped the door with flourishing importance. There was no answer to his knock though a few of the smaller boys standing safely out from the door began to whisper: 'She's staring out at us... She's upstairs... I seen the curtains moving... She's in... I seen her with my own two eyes.'

The door was rapped again, and this time the biggest boy hearing the shuffle of feet in the hallway, edged away from the door. The door was slowly opened, and before they could see her they chorused out: 'Could you please give us something for the bonfire?' She smiled at them and the smile drew their confidence, and they all crowded closer, each pleading with her to give them something.

'All right,' she said. 'Go round to the back-door and I'll give you something.'

They moved round dubiously. 'Maybe it's a bucket of water she'll throw round us!' the biggest said; and they all laughed — a laugh that was strange and low-pitched.

They heard the stiff bolt of the back-door scringing as she levered it back.

'There — would that be of any use for your bonfire?' she said pointing to a black sofa that was mottled with mildew and propped up with bricks to support a missing leg. They buzzed round it·where it lay under a sideless shelter, and in a few minutes had it hauled through the door and to the gable-end where they turned it over and examined it. Two coils of spring were bursting through the rust-stained sacking and a boy ripped them out, tied them to his feet with strings and began to walk round, shouting: 'The latest in stilts, boys! A walking jack-in-the-box!'

'Aw, give us a pair,' the young ones whined as the stuffing and springs were torn out of the sofa by the bigger boys. It was then that a half-crown jingled on the ground and one boy pounced on it.

'Finder is keeper!' he said and tried to put it in his pocket.

'No, you won't!'

'It's mine. I found it. I saw it first.'

'It's the oul' woman's,' they shouted, balked into honesty.

'Come on and we'll give it back to her,' the leader said.

'That's right! That's fair! Give it back to her!' they all chanted except the one who held the coin in his fist.

'All right,' he agreed dolefully, and they threw their caps in the air and went back with him to the old woman. They told her they found a half-crown in the lining of the sofa.

'Are you sure it's not your own?' she said.

'Naw, where'd we get a half-crown.'

She took the silver coin in her hand, turned it over, and stared at a small hole near the rim. She went out with them to the old sofa and they pointed to the exact place where the coin had fallen. For a moment she stood without speaking and the boy who had the springs tied to his feet disengaged them shyly, fearful that he had done something that had annoyed her.

'Keep the half-crown and buy sweets for yourselves,' she said quietly. They gave a cheer of delight, hoisted the sofa on to their shoulders like a coffin and marched off singing *The Boys of Wexford*.

As she stared after them a long sigh broke from her. She was trembling and she went into the house and sat near the fire in the kitchen. She gripped the arms of the rocking-chair to steady herself, and over and over again she said aloud: 'Calm yourself! Calm yourself!' for her mind was leaping back to a night, fifteen years ago, when her only son went out that door, never to come back. Where he went to she didn't know, and whether he was alive or dead she might never know. She had grown tired watching for the postman, and though letters came regularly from her two married daughters the letter she prayed for, never came.

Her tears flowed freely — tears of remorse and of baffled pity. One thing she now knew; she knew it now — her son had not lied to her when he swore he didn't steal his sister's half-crown. It was good to know that, though her home was broken on account of it and she was alone and had nobody to tell it to.

She shrugged her shoulders and poked up the fire. She could believe him now: believe him with all her heart and without forcing herself to believe. And if only he'd step into the kitchen this very moment, she'd go down on her knees and ask his forgiveness.

She sighed, put a hand to her forehead, and spoke aloud to herself: 'Ah, son, wherever you are this day, be you alive or dead, I believe you. You didn't steal the half-crown. It was

lying hid in the old sofa all these years. That's where it was —
in the old sofa!' She swayed to and fro, and the rocking-chair
creaked under her weight.

God in Heaven, she never could forget that night he
quarrelled with her and left the house. More than anything else
she thought about it. And not a morning passed and not an
evening passed but she prayed with all her might that he'd come
back.

But why hadn't she believed him when he swore he didn't
touch the half-crown. Oh, maybe she'd have done it if only her
daughters hadn't screeched and cried out against him. And the
language they used that night — it was scandalous! Language
they picked up in the factory and the mills — they didn't hear it
from her: at least she could say that for herself.

'But wait a minute, wait a minute,' she said aloud to her
own memory. 'Wait a minute till I get it all clear again.'

It was in the evening it all happened. And the first in from
work that evening was Mary and Anne. And what did they do
first: they tidied themselves at the jar-tub in the scullery while
I got their tea ready. They were in good form the pair of them.
They were singing and they were laughing, and each was urging
the other to hurry for they were going to see a picture in the
First House of *The Clonard.*

'And where are you getting the money from?' I asked them.

'We have it ourselves. We've a half-crown. There it is and
there's a hole in it for luck.'

It was Mary who took the half-crown from her apron-pocket,
the black shiny apron she used at work — and she laid the half-
crown on the mantelpiece beside the clock. It was beside the
clock she left it, for I remember when they discovered it was
gone they lifted up the clock and shook it, and they lifted up
the two brass candlesticks and the tea-canister. But it wasn't
there: it wasn't anywhere about the kitchen.

But wait now, wait now, I'm going too quick. What happened
after they left the half-crown on the mantelpiece. Let me see:
I made them their tea and I poured it out for them and sat on
the sofa watching them. I didn't lift the half-crown: I didn't
touch it; I didn't look at it to see the little hole that was in it
for luck. I am sure of that. I knew it was there on the mantelpiece for I heard it click the time Mary planted it down beside
the clock. And as I sat on the sofa I heard Jimmy's rat-tat at

the door. He came in and he, too, was in the best of form. I remember he was in a hurry out. He was a good boy, Jimmy, he loved a book and he wasn't using the house as a lodging-house like them two straps of girls. They were always on the go — two runners if ever there were ones: two clips of daughters that didn't give a straw whether I was left alone one night or two nights or every night. No, they didn't give a rap about me, but poor Jimmy did.

But I'm wandering again. Where was I? I was where Jimmy came in. He took off his oily linens and poured hot water into a basin in the scullery for him to wash himself with. Nothing could take the oily grease off him like hot water and washing-soda. The oily smell off his clothes was like the oil I used in the sewing-machine that made me sick. I remember he was singing. He used to sing one thing and another that he picked up at his work. But he always sang: *My feet are here on Broadway this blessed harvest morn* — he knew I liked that, for he knew that I was reared in a country parish that had seen many a decent girl and boy set off for America.

My mind's wandering on me again. Where was I? Yes, Jimmy washed himself in the scullery and I boiled a fresh egg for his tea. He didn't want any hot water for shaving for he said he wasn't going out. Merciful God, he wasn't going out! He said he was in no hurry for his tea and he'd wait till Mary and Anne had finished theirs. He lay on the sofa — his shirt was open at the neck and his face was red and fresh after the good washing he gave himself. I handed him his slippers that I had warming at the side of the hob and I lifted his working shoes to give them a brush or two for the morning. And then when the girls had finished their tea I cleared away the soiled dishes and asked Jimmy to sit over to the table. The girls were brushing their hair at that looking-glass on the wall.

'Where are you set for, the night? You're in a hell of a hurry,' Jimmy said.

'The pictures.'

'Who's taking you?'

'We're taking ourselves.'

'You must have plenty of spondulics when you can go every night in the week to the pictures.'

'It's our own money. We never see much of yours. You'd never ask us to the pictures — not if you got in for nothing.'

'I'd like my job taking you two anywhere.'

I disremember rightly what happened after that but I think Mary sat on the sofa and Anne went upstairs for her good coat from the back of the door and I went out to the yard for a shovel of coal. That coal was always damp and I mind the way it hissed on the fire and Jimmy saying he must put sides on that shelter in the yard. It was then that I seen Mary standing on the fender and looking on the mantelpiece and asking if I saw her half-crown.

'It's there beside the clock where you left it,' I said.

'It's not.'

She stood on a chair and lifted up the clock and looked under it and behind it.

'Did you take it, Mother?'

'I didn't lay a finger on it.'

Anne came into the kitchen with her good coat on, ready for the road. I don't know what happened next for my mind is all in a tangle. But I remember the both of them talking at once and asking Jimmy to fork up the half-crown and not be codding any more and keeping them late. Jimmy laughed and I thought by the way he laughed he was fooling them and hiding the money on them. They eyed the time by the clock and then they shouted at him to stop the bloody nonsense and give them the half-crown and not keep them late.

'I didn't touch it I tell you,' he said.

'You're a liar!' they shouted back at him, and I told them to hush and not let the next-door neighbour hear them fighting.

'You're a liar!' Mary shouted again, for she had a she-devil's temper when you roused her. She tapped her foot on the floor and glared at him.

'You put your collar-stud on the mantelpiece when you were going to wash,' she said. 'The stud's there for all to see but the half-crown's not!'

Jimmy put down his cup and smiled at her.

'Give it to them, son, if you have it, and don't keep them late,' I said.

'Didn't I tell you I never seen it!'

'You're a thief!' Mary screeched. 'That's what you are — a thief!'

Jimmy jumped up from the table then and struck her, for I remember Mary crying and expressions flying from her mouth

that'd have shamed any decent-minded girl. Oh, them factories
and warerooms is no place, let me tell you, to rear your children
in: they hear every filth and it sticks in their minds like grease
in an old pot. But I'm rambling again. I done my best to quieten
them and I told Jimmy he done wrong to hit her.

'I'll do it again if she calls me a thief!'

'You're a coward,' Anne said, 'only a coward would strike a
girl.'

Jimmy sat down again and I knew by the way his cup rattled
on the saucer that he was sorry for what he had done. I looked
under the square of linoleum near the fender for the half-crown
and I looked under the sofa, and I took the tongs and searched
in the ashes in the grate but I couldn't find it.

'It's no use looking for it,' Anne said. 'That playboy has it
well hid. Make him give it up to us.'

'Jimmy, son,' I said, 'give them the half-crown. It didn't
fly off the mantelpiece by itself.'

He stared at me and I'll remember that look to my dying day.

'So you don't believe me either. As sure as there's a God
above me I didn't take it.'

'You needn't bring God into it,' I said, for I was annoyed at
hearing him swear like that.

'He'd damn his soul over the head of it,' Mary shouted.

I don't know what made me do it, but I remember asking
Jimmy to turn out his pockets. Ah, God forgive me for asking
him to do the like of that! Sure I should have known he hadn't
it after he swore he hadn't.

He got up from that side of the table near the looking-glass
and he pushed in his chair slowly — I'll never forget that! He
went upstairs to his room and after five or six minutes of
rummaging and rumbling he came down the stairs and banged
the front door on his way out.

'Under God where is he away to?' I said.

'He's away to spend it,' Mary jeered.

I went upstairs to his room and I saw nothing behind the
back of the door only a bare coat-hanger, and on my downstairs I noticed his heavy overcoat was gone from the rack in
the hall.

'He's left us,' I said.

'He'd be good riddance if he did,' Mary said.

'He'll come back,' I said. "Jimmy's not the kind of boy

that'd run away from home".'

Little did I know then, and it fifteen years ago, that he wouldn't come back. Yes, indeed, fifteen long and lonesome years.

She rocked herself gently on the chair and began to cry. Then she dried her eyes in her apron and looked slowly round the cheerless kitchen. There was no light in it except the dull glow of the fire, and in the window space a blue sky sprinkled with stars. She shuddered, and as she leaned forward to lever up the coal in the grate there was a loud knock at the door that startled her. She rested the poker on the hob and waited. The knock came again. She hoisted herself from the chair, and as she walked down the hallway she heard the impatient shuffle of feet outside. She opened the door slowly and a few boys shouted breathlessly in at her: 'Hurry up, Missus, we're going to light the bonfire now.'

She hesitated for a moment in the hallway, and then pulling a shawl over her shoulders she made her way down to the middle of the street. The street lamps were in darkness and there was nothing but the tapping of feet, the mumble of unseen crowds, and a warm smell of paraffin. Boys, strangely dressed and their faces painted, were screaming like Indians and applying torches of paper to the heap of stuff they had collected. Then in a few minutes there came a hurl and burl of flame, a crackling of sticks, and a cheer from the crowd that drowned the noises of the fire. The flames lit up the faces and hands of the crowd and tilted their shadows on the red-brick house. Flames like flowing water sped over the old sofa, a bicycle tyre was a ring of flame, leafy branches of trees hissed in the heat, and a rubber boot entangled among the twigs furred with flame and dripped drops of fire from its writhing toe.

The old woman moved out from the heat with its sickening smell of paraffin, and stood in the cooler shadows cast by the outer ring of swaying onlookers. No one noticed her. They began to sing *Hail Queen of Heaven,* and when the singing came to an end a loud cheer volleyed above the houses, squibs banged in the fire, and a rocket gushed into the sky trailing behind it an arc of bright blue stars. The noise frightened the old woman and she hurried away from it. Near her home she looked back and saw the smoke lighted up by the fire and heard an accordeon playing an Irish reel. She didn't stop to listen to it.

She went into the house and halting in the hallway she clasped her hands and cried: 'Mother of God, are you listening to me! Wherever Jimmy is this night tell him that I believe him – tell him that from me!'

MICHAEL McLAVERTY was born in Monaghan in 1907 and taught for many years in Belfast. Summer holidays were spent in Rathlin, that half-way house between Ireland and Scotland where the Irish is half Ulster and half Scots-Gaelic and Bruce in exile met his spider. In the forties and fifties he wrote eight lyrical novels about his troubled province, reflecting his urban upbringing and island holidays. His people are gentle realists taking the sectarianism and bitterness in their stride and seeing neighbours as friends or enemies not in terms of their religion or politics but simply as people. His short stories which have made his name famous internationally are excellent in their evocation of youth and age, of reluctant city-dwellers dreaming of lost fields, of innocence and self-sacrifice and the finding of grace in an apparently unrewarding world. The story printed, one of two pieces written for *The Bell,* is perhaps sentimental in conception but in the intensity of the emotion and in its accurate rendering of working-class Belfast is well-worth reading.

A HALF-CROWN   Michael McLaverty   *August 1951*

THE BISHOP OF GALWAY
AND 'THE BELL'

By SEAN O'FAOLAIN

Sir,

A TRULY extraordinary address seems to have been delivered recently to a congress of University students in Galway — if the reports in the Press are accurate — by His Lordship, the Bishop of Galway. In the course of this address His Lordship singled out *The Bell* for special mention.

As I had the honour of being editor of *The Bell* for several years, was closely connected with it subsequently, have written for it on its revival, and wrote for it recently on the subject of the relationship of Church and State as we find it here in connection with a matter with which His Lordship was closely concerned, I can hardly do otherwise than take these references to *The Bell* as including me, if not directed against me. I must therefore reply.

I may well describe as extraordinary an Address, reasonably under the caption, BISHOP ON HOSTILITY TO THE CHURCH, which (in thus implicating a Catholic writer and journalist) declares that: 'For all *who have not faith* the Church was a human institution merely, and all the gradations of *bitter hostility, hatred,* or *mere indifference* that she evoked from the *fury* of the Orangemen of Sandy Row, to the *venom* of the *Irish Times* and the *rancour* of *The Bell, all* derived from a *refusal to see in her the divine.'* (My italics.) This, from a high dignitary of the Church means that I am publicly represented either as a venomous, hostile or rancourous anti-Catholic, or as one who — a later phrase from the Address — in 'ill-concealed hostility' to the Catholic Church co-operates willingly with people so inclined.

It is extraordinary because elsewhere there exists a more normal relationship between priest and people than this. Of this ordinary relationship Irish Catholics sometimes dream fondly, thinking with Saint Augustine, who said on a very famous occasion that even when harrassed or troubled by local events we should console ourselves with the thought of those 'living afar off and unknown'. He was saying, in effect, if I may put his thoughts into a familiar metaphor, that when a regiment finds the sergeant-major rather irksome the troops should think of other regiments, and other officers, and of the army as a whole, and suffer on for the King's sake. Otherwise there is nothing to do but ask for a transfer. I think it will be agreed that in England, France and Italy Catholic writers are treated with a trifle more of common Christian (or other) charity.

The Address is extraordinary because – in the context of its assault on those Catholics who, quite legitimately, maintain that the persistent and universal relationship between Church and State must perforce always be one of healthy tension – His Lordship appears to propose the extraordinary doctrine that the Catholic Church, being divinely appointed, is beyond and above all criticism. Indeed, His Lordship seems to propose that not merely is the Catholic Church thus divine but that all its members are divine – which a child at school knows not to be in accordance with the facts. Otherwise why should he assail *The Bell* for – ever so mildly, I may say – questioning the prudence of the ecclesiastical handling of the Mother and Child affair.

It is an extraordinary Address in which a Bishop, while thus bludgeoning down the most meek and mild criticism proceeds blandly to wonder, 'if anyone were satisfied that we had developed in Ireland a body of writers who understood the Catholic social ethic and could defend it with nerve and skill?'

Does His Lordship *really* want such writers? Or does he wish for propagandists whom any clever agnostic could pulverise in ten minutes? Are not such Addresses better calculated to reduce everybody to a cautious silence in public, and to moans and groans in private, beginning with, or ending with, 'If it wasn't for the wife and kids....'?

The moral of all this is that it is obviously impossible to develop a Catholic intelligentsia in any country where motives, instead of being respected, are immediately and persistently suspected; or where the attitude to the laity is that of Cardinal Manning's friend, 'Newman's most relentless enemy, Monsignor

Talbot, who said: 'What is the province of the laity? To hunt, to shoot, to entertain? But to meddle with matters ecclesiastical they have no right at all.'

Few Catholics here who have to consider their careers, not to speak of their wives and children, are going to stray far from Count Mosca's advice to the young cleric: 'Believe what they tell you, or not as you prefer, but never raise an objection. Imagine they are teaching you the rules of whist. And would you raise objections to the rules of whist?' His Lordship speaks bravely of the Church as the champion of Reason and Liberty. I believe that the universal Church is so, in a large and generous way. I believe that, in broad principles, the Irish army of the Church Universal stands firmly for Reason and Liberty. But no sooner does a practical issue arise here than....

This matter of Catholic writers is the test. Could a Graham Greene live here? A Mauriac, a Bernanos, a Peguy, a Mounier, a Pierre Emmanuel? Think of the things that Bernanos said about the Church in his Brazilian Diary! Which, by the way, was partially published in the Jesuit priodical *The Month* – in England. Can one imagine it appearing in *The Irish Monthly*? Or think of *Les Grandes Cimitières sous la Lune!* The thing is patent. Writers need a generous atmosphere to grow in. His Lordship is certainly helping to create it! I am afraid all His Lordship wants is abject compliance.

Yours truly,

SEAN O'FAOLAIN

'The Bishop of Galway and *The Bell*' was written in answer to a fairly severe attack upon such venomous and rancorous periodicals as *The Irish Times* and *The Bell*. The answer in its good manners and incorrigibility it was typical of the writer and *The Bell* at its best.

THE BISHOP OF GALWAY AND 'THE BELL'
Sean O'Faolain   *September 1951*

PROPHET
By ANTHONY CRONIN

When word came back to that small sun-drenched village,
Strange rumours of his ways and of his talk,
The neighbours shook their heads and didn't wonder,
His mother was bewildered more than proud.
And coming into darkened towns at evening,
Seeing the warm red gloom behind the blinds,
Lying awake in strange rooms above rivers,
He thought he would be like them if he could.
And when at last the courteous powers took notice
And nailed him to that awful point in time,
He knew that what he meant would be forgotten
Except by some as lonely as himself.

ANTHONY CRONIN was born in Enniscorthy, Co. Wexford in 1926 and educated in Trinity College, Dublin. He was a major contributor to *The Bell* and its associate editor from 1951. He lived in London for some years where he was Literary Editor of *Time and Tide,* later in Spain and now lives in Dublin. He is a noted poet, a fine if stringent critic and author of the satirical novel of Irish life, *The Life of Riley* (1964). He has published several books of critical essays including *A Question of Modernity* and his long poem, *RMS Titanic* was included in *The Penguin Book of Longer Contemporary Poems* (1966). He is a regular contributor to *The Irish Times* and a frequent broadcaster. His most recent book, *Dead As Doornails* (1976) is a memoir of his earlier literary life which contains noted portraits of Brendan Behan and J. MacLaren Ross.

PROPHET   *Anthony Cronin*   *17, 9 December 1951*

HAMLET IN ELSINORE
By MICHEÁL MacLIAMMÓIR

JUNE 8th: Woke suddenly and opened curtains onto balcony and a bright ghostly light: my watch said three o'clock and it is correct. The thought that there is virtually no darkness here gives me strange drafty *frisson*: I tell myself that this really is the North and indulge in flights of fancy about the Snow Queen (have brought Irish translation of Hans Andersen with me), though the map tells me we are only on a level with Dundalk: this, for no reason whatever, depresses me.

The castle of Kronborg so ubiquitous — on the right-hand side from my windows and in front of or behind one's eyes on every walk — that I didn't visit it until this evening. Hilton had worked there all day with Danish extras and at six there was a rehearsal for us all. The stage, built to Michael's design, enormous, and Coralie and I both happy for it will suit what unkind people call our Swooping Technique. Eithne, too, in spite of her smallness, seems at home and scuttles about like a rabbit: her mad scenes (excellent) should fit her for a Marathon Race. Nunnery scene and fencing match promise to give me a figure like Lennox Robinson but I'll have to use a bigger voice. Burning question of Mikes or no Mikes? Danish opinion sharply divided. Neither Gielgud or Olivier production used them, says one group. Neither could they be Heard, sharply retorts opposition. Personally loathe Mikes and all their fell associations, but on regarding the vast cold wind-ravished courtyard, northern Renaissance walls, distant green copper turrets, and ranks of far-away empty wooden benches, my loathing wavers. Final decision: we are to have a few, very discreet and placed, as somebody brightly suggests, "Just Here and There". (Precisely where else could they be placed?)

A letter from dear Fay Compton full of underlined words and unholy murmurings. Says she supposes I will dress, as John Gielgud did, in The Dungeon, and recalls the time when, dressed as Ophelia, she stood *outside* it (The Dungeon), singing carols to him in *streaming rain*. Was inspired by this to visit Dungeon, accompanied by Hilton as we are to share it, and found it luxurious if chilly, but am doubtless judging by Gate Theatre dressing-room standards. In fact the dreadful truth is dawning: I like the whole place and am smugly prepared to enjoy myself.

Impossible, however, to find a trace of Hamlet here: the real Hamlet. Was there one? As Shakespeare wrote him I suppose not, so assuredly not that this bleak negation as assuredly, I suppose, accounts for his absence from these walls. A pity, for I am naively eager to the sensing of ghosts in appropriate settings: long talks with Gráinne at Tara and Newgrange, rambles with Nero or Vittoria Colonna in Rome, a spirited crack with Miss Brontë at Haworth. But here, what can one do? In the garden of our hotel there is an early twentieth century statue of a neatly built young man with a vexed expression and a feathered hat much favoured by seagulls: "Hamlet" is inscribed underneath but one doesn't believe it. He makes a further stony appearance in a public park on the out-skirts of the town, incongruously stripped to the waist and wearing frilled trunks, as he gazes acrimoniously at an effigy of Ophelia in a sort of neo-Greek *négligé*, but one can't accept either of them. Georg Fleischman and camera very busy with us all as we gaze at these works; and further up on a green hill overlooking the town is a tombstone of Striking Viking appear-ance where they say he is buried. But it is the actors who have played him and the others who have supported them who really haunt the place.

June 9th: Dismay among the company because of the constant reappearance of Smorbrot at every meal. This national delicacy, spread on its myriad platters like an edible rainbow over vast linen-draped areas of table, is at first sitting (or rather standing, for one helps oneself) deliciously exciting, but certainly achieves a monotony almost as great as that of Bacon and Eggs in Our Own Islands when it confronts one twice a day, as well as a sort of infinitely varied monotony. The great trick I find is to select one, or at most two, dishes and stick to them. It is followed, and sometimes accompanied, by stewed fruit obscured by a sweet mayonnaise. Caustic Kay Casson has taken to saying "And now for some Smorbrot and Bryl-Cream Plums: Can't *wait,* my dear!" The fact that coffee afterwards is extra also causes havoc, though surely this is usual? Passionate speeches made about this with opposition mainly from Reg Jarman who grows eloquent in Tom Brown's Schooldayish fashion and says "Damn it all, we are *guests* in the country."

"Then why must we pay for coffee?" say the agitators but are firmly quelled by R. J. and supporters.

Spent entire evening fencing with Michael Laurence on the stage in howling gale. Peter Letts (Stage Director) expert and helpful, but neither M. L. or I were much good, M. probably would be if I were better, but the moment he gets in a lunge I howl for mercy.

June 11th: Répétition Génerale for critics only arranged for tonight but postponed owing to torrents of rain. All of them, I hear, furious, and sped scowling back to Copenhagen. Have developed rich raw-throated cold and sent for doctor. Also for bottle of Schnapps: drank it and played Surrealist Guessing Game all evening with Sally, Coralie, Pat McLarnon, Jack Jordan and the Cassons.

June 12th: Critics, clearly visible in spite of drizzle, sat in a wedge-shaped phalanx and seemed, by the majority of their facial expressions, pleased. Play went smoothly and it is oddly undisconcerting to see so plainly the audience's reactions. Coralie on top of her form in Closet Scene; Laertes and Horatio, from what I could gather, playing beautifully. I wished I could have seen Eithne in her mad scenes, but as McMaster says, No Hamlet has ever witnessed the mad scenes. ("When else are we supposed to get a rest, pray?")

Felt, in spite of cold, able for it all, but no doubt that damp grey evening light unbecoming. Felt extraordinary inspiration from the sky, even though the "brave o'erhanging firmament fretted with golden fire" was a hollow mockery. Whenever I felt lost, discouraged, and suddenly alone — a frequent sensation and one that, far from vanishing with the years, increases — I looked up and there it was, luminous, remote, yet indescribably reassuring, pressing down over turrets and battlements. At the end of the play, carried up the steps and across the upper rostrum by the four captains, I half-opened my eyes and saw it again: clouds dabbled with greenish light riven over

its clear spaces; the turrets and the battlements now in darkness
and the banners of Fortinbras dipping to the applause.

I shall never play the Nunnery scene as it should be played;
its meaning is still undefined to me. I waver between Hilton's
direction, the unwelcome influence of other performances, and
my own conflicting ideas.

June 13th: And Friday too! Yet Hilton, backed by Irish
actors and Danish producers, said fair things; I myself was not
satisfied.

Peter O'Neill's welcome face appeared suddenly like a harvest
moon, and he brought messages from Maureen Delany. The
wires included one that lifted my spirits and filled me with
nostalgia: "Welcome to Denmark Asta Nielsen." None of the
younger generation remembers even the name of the best-
known Danish actress of her day, but I do. I have stolen pennies
to witness her dark square fringe, her wide nervous mouth, her
restless sequin gowns in all those films, speechless, and
accompanied by a piano playing *Destiny* and *Roses of
September.* At a more reasonable age, too, I saw her picture,
silent, haggard and bizarre, but very memorable, of Hamlet.
Large and festive Banquet after show: all speeches and
Schnapps, (I find it is here spelt and pronounced as Snaps),
Ministers from all over Europe present, Danish Foreign Minister
eloquent in incredibly good English.

June 15th: Enormous luncheon given to entire Company in
charming house between Elsinore and Copenhagen and overlooking small virginal-looking lake with rushes and two white
boats. Danish husband, Irish wife, everyone the soul of friendliness. Had brisk, and to me, absorbing conversation with the
most attractive person in the room, elderly Irishwoman known
to me only as Aunt Rose. So Aunt Rose and I polished off a
bottle of Bordeaux and a mountain of strawberries and had
the affairs of this world and the next perfectly taped before
you could say Skol. Large serious Danish gentleman herded all
of us together after coffee and gave slow but admirable translation of three of the notices; all, in the main, flattering, thank
God!

"What's this one like?" says I, pouncing on fourth paper
lurking unpleasantly beneath Danish-English dictionary.

"Oh, this one is not so good. Two of them are not so good as
these," and he nervously waved the Enlightened Ones.

So to-night Hilton, Jack Jordan and I persuaded uncompromising-looking gentleman in hotel to do them all and were told some Hideous Things. One said I was "Meaningless," another one "Old," (just like that); another "Short and Stout." Now, really. Can only hope these libels will not appear in other translations but will remain, like Hamlet's grave, the property of Denmark.

Five out of the nine so far available, however, excellent, so we should be pleased; yet how much more potent is the depression of dislike than the uplift of approval.

Was presented this morning by Lord Mayor with gold medal bearing inscription:

> "Spectacula in Cronburga Helsingore."

Also my name, the date, and a red and white ribbon. Can now attend functions commanding Orders to be Worn. Also illuminated address, very flattering. "His brilliant performance," and almost certainly inscribed before B.P. was witnessed. But I feel happy about this.

June 16th: Arrival of Swedish papers: all so far good.

June 17th: Shower, beginning tentatively during first ghost scene, suddenly developed into hissing splashing determination during my almost favourite scene to-night: the first meeting with Rosencrantz and Guildenstern. (How could Olivier cut them out of his picture? They, more than Horatio or Ophelia, are the great revealing lights on his interior character). Rain and wind so violent by the time I reached "I have of late, but wherefore I know not, lost all my mirth," that we were officially stopped and luckily missed the irony of "This brave o'erhanging firmament". Resumed after quarter of an hour, clothes sopping and no means of drying them. (Fay is right about The Dungeon). Stage and rostrums like lakes and the Switzers sent on to mop up and strew everything with sawdust. This stuck to us wherever contact was established through rest of show.

June 18th: Repeat performance of Shower, at precisely same point in play. Are Gerry Healy and Jim Kenny Voodoo rain-gods disguised as Rosy and Guildy? Chance of resuming work abandoned as after five minutes of playful deluge beginning on the lines "the air bites shrewdly, it is very cold," the heavens opened at the mention, some half an hour later, of the "brave o'erhanging firmament", and when we had cowered for ten more minutes under archways, it was clear that the cause was lost. Audience dismissed with sorrow (not one member of it had budged during the action of the play except to open umbrellas) and Coralie, the Cassons and I made our way through crowds of still hopeful and strongly autograph-minded lingerers to a car which bore us off to the Movies, where we saw *Strangers in a Train* with Danish sub-titles.

June 19th: Played in Gales of wind that would have satisfied Emily Brontë herself: amazing walk home alone after the show; sky torn and rent with flying clouds, the sea a livid opal.

June 20th: Pillar of resentful fire descended on us all in windswept but dry beer garden where Denis Brennan, having received letter and Irish cuttings from his wife Daphne, showed us the latter and we discovered that Our Newspapers (Sunday ones being the most emphatic) had with incredible diligence printed the cream (or scum) of all the bad *Hamlet* notices and made no Mention of any of the others. This, coupled with fact that one of the best had been quoted out of context so as to appear unfavourable, convinced us all that many of our friends at home were anti-Denmark or anti-Gate or perhaps both, and ensuing inquest took form of rapid and maledictory litany. Cuttings shown in silence to Heads and Fronts of Kronborg Festival who assumed Medusa expressions and unhesitatingly sat down to concoct protest in English which will keep them busy, I imagine. Attitude at home to our coming here has been mysterious from the start: now some of the mystery seems to be on the point of revealing itself, to us at any rate, if not to the public. Quote to myself Yeats' poem wrongly entitled "The People", also several lines from "John Bull's Other Island", and derive a certain ashy-tasting satisfaction. Strange, how after twenty-four years of work preceded by life-time of preparation for it should create such hostility; but am curiously glad instead of sorry that it is a little late now to turn back from the Irish road and do what everyone else has done.

The intellectuals of Dublin, most of whom are half-educated — or, like myself, not educated at all — have made in Ireland a paradise for students and amateurs of the drama and a living inferno for the mature artist, except of course where the public is concerned, and the public is as suspect as the success that it and only it can give to the theatre.

The Irish writer of English, practising his art and drawing

his inspiration where and whence he will, and reaping the fruits of his labour at a future time and probably in some distant land, has no such gloomy problem. At the worst his book, having appeared and been duly banned by his compatriots, is still in existence; he can fish it out of a drawer or refer to his British or American readers to bear witness to what he has done.

But with the actor it is different: we are born at the rise of the curtain and we die with its fall, and every night in the presence of our patrons we write our new creation, and every night it is blotted out forever; and of what use is it to say to audience or to critic "Ah but you should have seen me last Tuesday?"

To-day enlivened by visit in rattling private bus to the Tuborg Brewery. All its officials seemed to know English alarmingly well and we were conducted by one of them through a sea of flashlight photographers (more journalists!) and over impeccable wilderness of vats and test chambers and electrical diagrams and fermenting rooms and stairways and distillery departments and halls full of stolid blue-bloused blondes of both sexes, of whirring machinery, of processions of madly waltzing bottles, and all permeated by an astringent smell of Hops (or whatever it is). Crystal-clear and elementary explanation of entire process in faultless English bewildered me more than ever: could only see it all as setting for play by Georg Kaiser or as background for death on dizzy heights of master criminal (Cagney or Welles or who you will). Individual reactions on company interesting: Hilton and Reg Jarman absorbed, Coralie and Sally staggering from the malt and hop-laden air and vaguely pleased with everything, Paul Farrell moo-ing louder than ever, Eithne, diamond-eyed on a gracious little cloud, Kay and Pat McLarnon frankly incredulous ("They're only doing it because we're tourists, dear") and Chris Casson, completely *hors da lui*, executing frenzied dance in the manner of trolley-whirled bottle. Lunch followed and we all made speeches. Copenhagen re-visited: wholly admirable and, like Brussels, a model for any small capital, showing how agreeable life can be made even in a sub-human climate.

Later. Hamlet, incomparable, as the world knows, as a part, is yet too complicated for the actor's mind. We are one-dimensional, and, for the most important moment of our lives, for our work, inclined to mistake some curious isolated angle of existence for the whole, and give an incomplete and distorted version of our discoveries. We look at a statue as if it were a picture painted flat on a canvas: Hamlet is a statue and the average fine part a canvas. Have felt this, with increasing distaste for my own performance and most others, ever since I began to play him.

Yet his philosophy is elementary, when you divorce it from its utterance, his manners appalling, his method of detecting a crime not only ponderously elaborate but lacking in taste; his wit, like so much wit, a mere ferreting-out of other people's weaknesses. Probably much even of his mystery would vanish if Shakespeare had taken the trouble to write in some stage-directions. Still, he remains the sorcerer of the stage, and we all go on playing him too long for the excellent reason that we can't bear to leave him alone.

All is grey and murky outside; an evening like a badly developed photograph, the coast of Sweden a long despairing smudge: Hilton and I went there together and found another tall bright new town built round an ancient castle, a razor-edge of a wind, *Smorbrot,* and the names over the shops spelt a little wrong to our Danishised eyes.

June 22nd: No performance for two nights because, after dubious April weather all day, the twilight brings storms of rain. Our courtyard a sorry sight with its rows of waiting benches, its knots of frustrated playgoers, its domes rearing their heads against the downpour. And Michael O'Herlihy's canvases shuddering under a sixty-mile hurricane. *No more, No more!* moan the gulls. *No more!* cry the swallows. *No more.*

I am ill and have had to leave the Farewell Banquet: below me they are all raising their glasses and shouting Skol and glancing twice. For me I can only sit and write. Some day I will write about this episode: I can write only about places or people if I feel affectionate towards them, and that is how, in spite of a climate worse than our own, I feel about Denmark and its people.

                                        MICHEÁL MacLIAMMÓIR

MICHEÁL MacLIAMMÓIR was born in Cork in 1899 and spent his life in dedication to Ireland and Irish theatre. He toured the country with his

famous brother-in-law, Anew McMaster, in 1927, helped found An
Taibhdhearc, the Gaelic theatre in Galway City and began in partnership
with his lifelong friend, Hilton Edwards, the Gate Theatre, as an alterna-
tive venue for drama in the capital. His work for theatre included, acting,
designing and writing of plays, notable among which are *Ill Met by Moon-
light* (1954) and *Where Stars Walk* (1962). In the sixties he assembled
perhaps his best and certainly most popular theatrical pieces. *The
Importance of being Oscar, I Must be Talking to my Friends,* and *Talking
About Yeats.* These monologues, compiled and acted by himself and
directed by Hilton Edwards gave him world-wide fame and allowed him
to act as a kind of unofficial Irish ambassador. His most famous role as
an actor was as Robert Emmet in Denis Johnston's *The Old Lady Says
'No'* but his various Hamlets were just as impressive and he was a great
Iago to Orson Welles' Othello. His first volume of autobiography, *All for
Hecuba* (1946) first appeared in parts in *The Bell.* The piece printed here
is from his Diaries and tells with typical wit and heightened drama the
details of a characteristic Edwards-MacLiammoir adventure: playing
Hamlet not only on the Dane's own sod but in the actual castle in which
those bloody acts are said to have occurred. He died in 1978. At his
funeral his partner said, 'Ireland has lost a great Irishman who loved his
country in peace and served her in peace, not without honour and
distinction beyond her shores.'

HAMLET IN ELSINORE   Micheál MacLiammóir   *October 1952*

THEATRE

By VAL MULKERNS

IN the greatest of Elizabethan tragedies, Hamlet's the thing, not the play, or the staging, or anything else. The mind of Hamlet, with its astonishing and soaring cosmic range, is what occupies the evening, and what has occupied scholars, fidgety and otherwise, for almost three-hundred years. Everybody knows the theories, from Coleridge's vision of the sickly intellectual, incapable of action, to the Freudian concepts of a youth with an Oedipus complex who is unable to kill his uncle for killing his father because that is what he would like to have done himself, like perhaps, most of the theories, and little more than the recreation of men who might have been more usefully employed playing cricket, but their abundance at least demonstrates that the mind of Hamlet is vaster and more complex than that which any dramatist before or after Shakespeare ever dared to fit within the frame of a play.

The production which Dublin saw at the Olympia in July showed the final blossoming of the boughs that tossed a little uneasily about in Cork last May. The Danish tour came in between, and with it one guesses, a sharpening and brightening of the instruments that combined to make the Dublin presentation the thing of sheer beauty it was. For here was an occasion when even the critics Mr. Edwards has sometimes assaulted joined their voices the following morning in a psalm of praise. No other reaction was possible, except

apparently in certain Danish quarters. Setting, music, costumes, timing, interpretation, all fused for once in one clear blaze of intensity that will be spoken of most likely in Dublin as long as theatre is spoken of. It is difficult to remember the Mousetrap scene without also remembering the glorious and daring interplay of colour on a Gozzoli canvas where royal scarlet and purple and black and gold spread themselves lavishly under a Renaissance sun. The final stark holocaust to death is not softened but intensified by the brilliant swirl of the Norwegian banners and the occupying army's triumphant march onto the stage to the sound of martial music, and the glitter of drawn bayonets. I can never understand why producers so often like to drop their curtain on Hamlet, peaceful at last in Horatio's arms, the rest being silence. Edwards did this in Cork, but Shakespeare knew better, and Edwards has learned. The arrival of Fortinbras, like the knocking at the gate in *Macbeth*, is life flowing back again over destruction, as life always will. And when the dead Hamlet is borne up by four captains to the battlements and the audience sees the royal inverted face, it feels the full Sophoclean impact of the destruction of a great man, observed even by Fortinbras:

'Let four captains
Bear Hamlet like a soldier to the stage;
For he was likely, had been put on,
To have proved most royally.'

Micheál MacLiammóir, indeed, in his greatest role, proved most royally. I thought him very fine in Cork, but the Dublin performance plumbed wells of technical perfection, and brushed at times against the stars in a manner that was astonishing. This Hamlet is a creature of rare and fastidious intelligence. The trouble about the Ghost's injunction is that it is too simple. Simple killing is the act of a savage; the execution of precise justice is the business of Renaissance man, and so when Claudius at prayer was not killed, there was no question of mere procrastination. Mac Liammóir revealed this by the swift animal stride with drawn sword, the equally swift reaction of the mind— 'This would be scanned'. The alert questioning eyes showed you the scanning, the hardening white face revealed the merciless but just resolution. All through the play one was conscious of the mind rigidly in control, even (and MacLiammóir did this superbly) when confronted with the tide of his own passion for Ophelia: the open hands are for a moment helpless, poised to close about the girl, but again the white face hardens and the mind takes over.

All this may suggest that his Hamlet is without humanity, and if so, it would be wrong. Mac Liammóir's Hamlet is a very human person. The soul of a child who adorned two people at court, his father, and Yorrick, stands bare in the words: 'My father, methinks I see my father,' and in: 'Here hung those lips that I have kissed I know not how oft. Where be your gibes now? your gambols? your songs?' Again when the players arrive at court to the sound of thin fantastic music, it is, in a flash, not the tortured son of a murdered father who welcomes them, but Hamlet the student, whose subject was philosophy but whose love was the theatre. Speaking with them, and chaffing 'my young lady' he is transformed, a charming lively man excited at the prospect of pleasure, and determined that these humble people will be well bestowed, and that no snobbish old buffer will prevent it. Human too is the unworthy

vicious delight he takes in stripping a weaker mind than his own, leaving the various rash intruding fools to wriggle on the ground at his feet after the mental jujitsu. Those among the audience who brought with them a sweet romanticized conception of the Prince, cannot have gone away satisfied.

Taken all in all, this portrayal of Mac Liammóir's is a major one, comparable only to Gielgud's. Olivier's does not fall into the same category at all, being too close to the gentle, tender prince of Goethe's not Shakespeare's imagination. One is grateful that an actor of Mac Liammóir's stature chose to ignore the bright lights and the fat box offices and stay at home stubbornly and often thanklessly working with his partner to build up in Dublin a theatre at once native and in the wildest sense European. His curiously many-sided art could have fulfilled itself in many more profitable directions, were it not that (fortunately for Dublin) he was hag-ridden, and the hag was called Cathleen, the daughter of the obscure person, Houlihan.

If I have not left much space to deal with the other portrayals, it is not because they don't deserve it. Seldom can such a distinguished group have formed itself about a great actor before in Dublin. Hilton Edwards was a superb Claudius, a trapped and magnificent lion lashing his cloak about him like a tail, and also, at one moment, a broken and frightened man appalled by the realisation of his own guilt. Coralie Carmichael validly decided that Gertrude was a libidinous fool and no Clytemnestra, and cleverly tilted her performance to that angle. Christopher Casson's Polonius rivalled his own marvellous Uncle Vanya, and Patrick Bedford (who will learn later not to let the Liffey course quite so defiantly through his voice) Paul Farrell, Robert Hennessy, Gerard Healy, and Patrick McLarnon were all admirable. The praise that Eithne Dunne's Ophelia drew forth everywhere was merited. His performance was full of beauty, through which the elegiac note struck very early on. This Ophelia was a child friendless and bewildered into madness, whose one hope of hapiness was taken from her as casually as if it had been a toy. I particularly liked also Denis Brennan's handling of Horatio, a lovely rounded portrayal warm with real affection.

Earlier on in the season, Lord Longford presented Fry's *Venus Observed* — which Olivier fittingly treated in London as if it were a firework — and a sadly guttering candle it was indeed, as Dublin saw it. Then came a delightful *Lady Windermere's Fan*, full of speed and grace, and then *The Three Sisters*, to my mind this company at its very best. Dan O'Connell's production was leisurely and sure, and the settings by Alpho O'Reilly were rich in muffled suggestions of Moscow from which the Prozorovs have come, and can never quite forget it. Moscow is the pipedream of this little islanded group in a provincial town. They must suffer in this limbo for a time before they go to Moscow — suffer for three months, four perhaps? On Irena's saint's day when somebody gives her a samovar, and somebody else a book he has previously given her last Easter, it doesn't seem so far away, and the officers are here anyhow to while away the time, and Prozorov will be offered a chair at Moscow University. Doesn't everybody know how clever he is, and that he will never marry a woman who doesn't know what belt goes with what dress? So the social pattern emerges and Chekhov suggests in a dozen different ways that we are mutes or audience to a dying world, a doomed aristocratic tradition. The officers argue endlessly about the future — whither are you going, O Russia of mine? — and one is reminded of the morning-rooms of Turgenev agitated by the same winds, Tolstoy's palaces in which the first faint warnings are sounded; are there not peasants who refuse to load a carriage, serfs who neglect to grovel when spoken to? And always there are the Bazarovs, the handful of men in advance of their time to whom nobody will listen. But with Chekhov the general is reduced to the particular, and it is the crumbling

of personal relationships against crumbling social foundations that occupies him. Prozorov marries the lady with no sense of colour, and little of any kind, because she is young (he says) and he loves her, but in two years it is clear even to him that Moscow University will never know him, and that Natasha is merely an unpleasant bore. His sister Olga who would have married anybody 'good' becomes wedded instead to her school, and Masha, married to an insufferably cheerful schoolmaster, is disrupted by her passion for an officer whose wife frequently attempts suicide just to annoy him. The little Irena, the one uncrushed thing at the opening of the play, has found no solution in hard work, and no road to Moscow, and decides to marry the kindly silly Baron just before he is shot dead. So everybody fails everybody else, and the only happy people are the bourgeois schoolmaster and the old nurse, symbol of the new ruling class.

Iris Lawlor, who at one time I thought had the same formula for every character, a loud, high bounce, was a magnificent Masha, full of ice and fire, and Denis Edwards, Aiden Grenell, Charles Mitchell, Gervaise Matthews, and Dermot Tuohy were all at the top of their form, which is very high indeed. A special word of praise must go to Helena Hughes for a quietly sustained performance of great beauty. One or two of the others, I thought, were not quite in step, but on the whole *The Three Sisters* was a production of which any company might be proud.

The above note was already in proof when the strike hit us, and prevented the appearance of our August and September numbers. To avoid confusion next month it is necessary to deal briefly now with four other presentations. After Chekhov, Longford Productions in association with Maurice O'Brien, gave us Lord Longford's *The School for Wives*, less a translation of Moliere than a daring and successful transplantation. It was a delight, better even than its first production some years ago. Lord Longford handles his rhymed couplets with the poise and grace of a good juggler, and some of his more outrageous rhyming is infinitely funnier than Fry's similar efforts with Anouilh's *Ring Round the Moon*. The spirit of Moliere emerges glittering and intact. Incidentally Maurice O'Brien indicated once and for all that his genius is a comic one. His Amolphe was a magnificent piece of work. .

The *Othello* which followed this production was a surprising disappointment, despite Dan O'Connell's admirably swift handling. The main reason for its failure was Godfrey Quigley's inability to carry the colossal weight of Othello. His performance was slight, full of intelligence, and utterly unmoving. Helena Hughes' Desdemona was a delicately tragic domestic figure, but Desdemona is very much more. Miss Hughes' portrayal made utterly impossible, for instance, the dying words, "Nobody: I myself; farewell." After a sprawling and crude opening, Denis Edwards developed into a likely Iago, and did give the feeling, as Iago ought to do, of shaping the course of the play inside his own brain, driving it relentlessly (and also causelessly) towards tragedy.

After a most welcome revival of M. J. Molloy's *The King of Friday's Men,* the Abbey presented Walter Macken's new play *Home is the Hero*. A first production in these cautious days is always an event; not, as it happened, a very exciting event. Mr. Macken is a capable man of the theatre who is intimate with every possibility, every limitation, of his medium, and his new play is as shapely a piece of work as one would expect. But the new living material of the Galway slums never at any point becomes transmuted into

drama because the creative imagination that shapes it never musters it. O'Casey's slumdwellers differ from Macken's in that they are wholly absorbed by a creative imagination that never falters, never weakens for a moment into the mere reproduction of life, and reproducing the life around him as a camera might is no more the business of the dramatist than of the novelist.

Taken then, as it must be, on the low level of reportage, *Home Is the Hero* presents a handful of recognisable, sharply-observed human beings, and encircles them with a safety belt of familiar Abbey "characters", who bicker, make love, get drunk, grow affectionate, cool, and attempt to break one another's heads, to the delight of a large laughing audience. Paddo, the hero home from gaol, is the only character whose behaviour does not strike one as inevitable, and his final escape from the joys of domesticity into the homeless night is not convincing. Paddo on the whole, in fact, is a shaky foundation on which to build a play, and Brian O'Higgins is responsible for what judgment one is prepared to suspend during the course of the action. For the rest, the cast of nine serves the dramatist well, particularly Máire Ní Catháin, Eileen Crowe, Liam O'Foghlú, and Harry Brogan, whose Dovetail fits him like a glove which may quite possibly have been made to measure. Ria Mooney's hand is firmly felt all the time, helping both cast and dramatist over two or three moments that might well have shattered verisimilitude.

Lack of space prevents more than a reference to Ram Gopal's unforgettably beautiful Indian Ballet which the enterprise of Messrs. Ilsley and McCabe brought to the Olympia in August.

VAL MULKERNS was born in Dublin in 1925, educated by the Dominicans in Eccles Street and afterwards became in fairly quick succession a junior civil servant, a free-lance journalist, a teacher of English to foreigners and associate editor of *The Bell* (enough to make Joyce's father seem a stick-in-the mud). While in *The Bell* offices she wrote drama criticism, book-reviews and some stories and general articles. She wrote two novels in the early Fifties, *A Time Outworn* (1951) and *A Peacock Cry* (1954). In between she married Maurice Kennedy. They have two boys and a girl. Since then she has been fiction reviewer for *The Irish Times* and TV critic for *The Evening Press* (since 1968). In 1978 her first book for twenty years, a masterly collection of linked short stories, *Antiquities* was published. Another collection is expected in 1979. The piece printed is a review of the MacLiammoir Elsinore Hamlet which was put on in the Gate Theatre.

THEATRE   *Val Mulkerns*   *October 1952*

SOMEONE

By EWART MILNE

Someone pressed a button,
Someone pulled a trigger,
Someone was playing Patience,
Someone was reading the Holy Bible,
Someone was meeting someone at the old crossroads,
Someone was undressing for a bath,
Someone lay sleeping in the shade,
Someone sleeping had fallen slack
Who never knew he died.
I remember it very well.

They told me about it,
It was once upon a time;
And about someone who was a gardener,
But the rain washed all the soil away
And he threw down his fork and spade.
I remember it very well,

Once upon a time, it was,
And a good time coming, too,
When the Jew was made the scapegoat—
But it's different now humanity is the Jew.
Still I remember it very well.

And how someone ran into a cave to find the moon—
Lugh, the sungod, strangled him on a fallen town—
And someone, and it couldn't have been no one,
Said he'd seen afar the risen sail of Venus,
And heard, borne landward on the breeze,
Her harps and grand pianos.
They told me about,
Far away and long ago;
Still I remember it well,
Don't you? It was someone.

CHARLES EWART MILNE was born in 1903 in Dublin and though
he has been in his time a student teacher, a seaman and a journalist he is
best described simply as a poet. He has had fourteen books of poetry
published, the most recent being *Cantata Under Orion* (1977). 'Someone'
is one of nine poems printed in *The Bell*. Apart from poetry his greatest
interest is in science fact and he is a member of the British Interplanetary
Society. He lives in Bedford.

SOMEONE   *Ewart Milne*   *November 1952*

MILLSTONES
By MARY BECKETT

NELLY McGuinness was the good holy blessed saint in our street until she became the tortured lost soul. Now she's the laughing-stock of the place. Not that I ever laugh at her. Oh dear no. I've got to keep my reputation safe. I never say a bad word about anybody. I'd stand up for Herod himself. Being the only one in the street with a bit of education I can't let myself down. There's nobody really friendly with me but I'm not to have them sheering off altogether. It was to make Nelly McGuinness jealous of me that I worked for the scholarship to the convent.

I used to sit in school when we were in the seventh class and all I'd want to do was pinch her and nip her and trip her up with my foot stuck out between the seats, I wanted to make her shout out. Anything to shake her, she was so quiet and deep. She had black hair, straight shining black hair and her face was white, creamy-white not blue-white like the ones that didn't get enough to eat. She was serious and calm until she'd smile now and again, very slowly first, then she'd get a bit pink and her eyes would brighten up and sparkle. I used to watch the teacher saying things to try and make her smile and then just looking at her. She wasn't very smart at her books but nobody ever scolded her though they were never off my back.

Then she was talking of going away to be a nun. Oh, she couldn't wait till her parents saved the money. She was so eager that there were collections taken up for her in the street and in the mill, to buy her the clothes. But she never saw the inside of a convent. She saw Jerry Tobin first. And she's never seen anybody else since. Even now when he's making a fool of her in front of her own children she doesn't seem to notice.

I don't know what he ever saw in her; she might as well have
been a statue for all the life that was in her. But there he'd
be just like the teacher working away to get her to smile at him
and staring at her as if no girl had ever smiled at him before.
And he could have had any girl in the parish for he was big and
broad and golden like somebody in technicolour. His hair and
his eyes and his skin were all that queer golden shade, the
colour of a dusty street in a stormy sunset. Oh he had only to
give a jerk of his head and half the girls were laughing up into
his face. Once he noticed Nelly McGuinness that finished.

I know what the old women said: "Any man wants a good
woman for a wife no matter how many cheap girls run after
him." Jerry didn't know what the word good meant. I
remember the talk there was in the street the time his mother
died. We were only kids at the time but we heard them all
saying his father had killed her, beating at her with his crutch.
He had got his leg off in a ship in the East somewhere, and came
home with nothing to do but get roaring drunk on his pension.
Jerry was the same; there was a right thick streak of his father
in him. He was away half time in the home and then he was
put in gaol for sticking a knife in Larkie Holland's ribs. Oh,
no. It wasn't goodness Jerry was looking for.

But Nelly thought it was. It was as good as a play to watch
her beside him at Mass. She'd kneel in that still way that was no
effort to her. Her head would be a bit on one side and her lips
just breathing. Praying away, you might think until you'd see
her give the lick of a glance up from under her big black
eyelashes at Jerry beside her. If he was looking at her the pink
would creep up her cheeks and she'd give a kind of a quiver but
the beads would keep on going through her fingers. Not a
prayer did she ever say if he was there. Still she told me at that
time, that it was a puzzle to her to know what to tell in Confession for she never had time to commit any sins. She was
sleekit with herself, sleekit with God. I would dearly have loved
to tell her what she was with her conceit in herself and her pose
as a holy woman and the way she was going to pierce poor
Jerry's thick-skinned soul with her good example. A shining
light, a pink and white saint in glazed tiles in the corner of the
Church and Jerry Tobin on his knees before it!

But I had a guard on myself even then. Other women could
be jealous of her and say what they liked but I had been to the

high school, and had a job in the office of a shop. I was a young lady so I wasn't supposed to want the same things as mill-girls; I had no right to be jealous. I wasn't jealous anyway. I just hated her close face and the way she would hold on to Jerry's arm, and her four yellow children.

Then he left her. God knows why. One Friday night he didn't come home, and the next any of us heard of him he was up in court in Liverpool for slashing a man in a pub with a broken bottle. Four years he was given. Nelly had no money. Right enough I was sorry for her. So was everybody and we took up another collection. But anybody else would have gone out to work. Nelly didn't. She just stayed at home nursing her baby until she got her notice to leave the house. There was no door open to her. Most of the houses were far too crowded anyway and more and more workers were being paid off every week. Even so she had no right to come and ask me to take her in just because I had the house to myself. Always so sweet with me she was but she was bound to have known I hated her. She spent the first night in a shed on the brickfield. She spent the next five years with Tom O'Rourke, a widower with two children. He has three more now.

You'd have expected her to shrivel a bit, to let herself sag. But she looked prouder and straighter than ever. She didn't pretend to be anything but what she was. She carried the weight of sin around with her the way slave-women carried pitchers of water on their heads. I had a jug and basin belonging to my mother with figures like that on the outside. I smashed it.

I wasn't the only one. Willie Mason next door to me had his eye on her. The first time I noticed it was at the party the night after his wife's fifth baby was born. The kitchen was hot and full of smoke and there wasn't room to breathe. Willie was down on his hands and knees playing with two of the children. They were blowing fizz into his face. He had a soft face — soft and red and damp. One of the women nudged another and tipped him over with her foot and he sprawled on the floor and we all laughed at him until his mother-in-law shouted at him to get up and stop making a fool of himself. She was trying to squeeze round to give us all red jelly and baker's iced buns.

Nellie was sitting with her head leaning back against the wall. He scrambled up and went and stood beside her and his hand pressing down on her shoulder and whispered in her ear. She

might have been blind and deaf for all the notice she gave him.
He let on he didn't care. He went over to Rita Holmes, a fat
blonde girl and she kept on giggling at him and then taking
every odd look in at his wife lying in the room off the kitchen
with a scrawny dark-haired child on her arm.

He never let her alone from that, shouting after her from the
street corner, following her when she was by herself, spitting
out when she went by. All the time she paid him no heed but
passed quietly up and down the street. She was frightened of
him though. I could see it in her eyes. And she had reason too.
When Tom O'Rourke's pay couldn't keep their combined
families any longer she went into Hoey's mill at the foot of the
street. Willy Mason got a job there too. The women said it was
terrible to watch him the way he persecuted her. But there was
nobody there when he pushed her over the loom.

It was the day the workers got off for the "Twelfth" week. I
rcalled in on my way home to see how Nelly was enjoying the
party. I was nice and clean and neat and they were dirty and
rowdy with their hair in curlers. They told me she must be
upstairs. I slipped up and there she was lying moaning and Willy
Mason kicking at her and shouting at her to "get up, get up for
God's sake". She had her eyes closed and she was white and I
thought to myself "Now Blessed Nelly Tobin will go roaring
down to Hell". Neither of them saw me. I tiptoed out again
down through the yard. The women were laughing and dancing
round in their leather aprons with their tools clanking, singing
"Roll out the Barrel" and waving their bottles over their heads.

I might have known she was a fraud and a hypocrite then
too. It turned out she had nothing wrong with her but a couple
of broken ribs. Anyway it brought Jerry running back home to
her again. He took her back without a word against her and
her whole gang of children and got a house in the next street
when nobody else can even find a room. And there he is
behaving like a besotted fool over her again.

I watched the pair of them going to Confession last Saturday
night, poor Jerry embarrassed, tripping against the kneeling
board of his way in and out of the seat and pushing the Con-
fessional door instead of pulling it. But not Nelly. When she
came out she smiled back at Jerry. Her eyes were shining and
she was covered with blushes as if it was an innocent young
girl. Friends all round her again now she has. I didn't bother

going into the box myself. I went out of the Church behind
them. They walked home hand in hand together. Hand in
hand, God help us!

I had Annie, their eldest girl laughing about them on Sunday,
when I brought her in for a cup of tea. As she said herself:
"The whole thing would fair disgust you".

MARY BECKETT was born in Belfast in 1926, educated at St.
Dominic's High School and St. Mary's Training College, which stand side
by side on the Falls Road. She taught in Ardoyne for ten years from 1946
to 1956 when she married and went to live in Dublin. She has had stories
published in *Threshold, Irish Writing* and had others broadcast on BBC
and RE. In all six of her stories were published in *The Bell* between 1951
and 1954. She writes accurately and darkly but with great compassion
about the poorer people of her native city and of the politically speckled
countryside where the grandparents of her city characters once lived in
uneasy truce with the opposite sect. Now that her five children are well
reared she has begun to write again.

MILLSTONES   *Mary Beckett*   *February 1954*

INDEX OF CONTENTS

187

INDEX OF AUTHORS